FAMILY FEARS

Also available by these authors:

Creative Grandparenting (Discovery House, 1992)

FAMILY FEARS

JACK & JERRY SCHREUR

VICTOR BOOKS

A DIVISION OF SCRIPTURE PRESS PUBLICATIONS INC.
USA CANADA ENGLAND

The illustrations in this book are of real families. Their stories have been changed and at times composites have been used to protect their privacy and confidences.

Scripture quotations are from the *Holy Bible, New International Version*®. Copyright © 1973, 1978, 1984 by International Bible Society. Used by permission of Zondervan Publishing House. All rights reserved.

Copy Editors: Mary Sytsma & Greg Clouse

Cover Designer: Scott Rattray

Cover Photo: Comstock

For my Grandma and Grandpa Schreur

Who never gave up hoping and praying for my Dad,
and never let their fear control them.

CONTENTS

PART ONE

Who's Afraid
of the Big Bad Wolf?

CHAPTER ONE

Tales from the Dark Side

S andra couldn't figure her father out. At one time they
had been very close, but then she started dating Craig
and her dad seemed to change right before her eyes. He
was always asking her when she would be home, and when
she got home he would quiz her for twenty minutes about
where she had been.

Then, tonight, she was half an hour late. Her father was
waiting at the door. "Sandra, you're late. I can't believe you
would do this to your mother and me."

"What do you mean, Dad? I'm just late."

"You know very well what I mean. You and Craig, I know
what you were doing. Don't try to pretend with me. I'm not a
fool, you know."

"Dad, I wasn't even with Craig. I was with Michelle, and we
were having so much fun that we just forgot about the time.
What is wrong with you? Why are you so upset?"

"Sandra, I know what is going to happen to you and Craig. I
don't want you seeing him. You'll end up just like your
sister!"

With that Sandra's dad turned around and, without waiting
for an explanation or a reply, walked out of the room. Sandra
went to bed crying, wondering what was happening to her

11

relationship with her dad, wondering why he was so cold and why he thought so little of her.

Her dad didn't sleep that night. All he could think of was his oldest daughter, three years older than Sandra. He couldn't forget the night she had come home with tear-stained cheeks and red eyes. "Dad, Mom, I'm pregnant." Oh, how those words had hurt. How disappointed and embarrassed he was. He didn't know what to do. He had let his wife say soothing words of encouragement while he tried to control his anger. In the end he lost that battle, blurting out some of the most terrible and hurtful things any father could say about his own flesh and blood. Susan had run crying from the house. He didn't see her for six months. She had an abortion, moved in with her boyfriend, and broke off all contact with her family.

Now he spent his nights almost paralyzed with fear that his prized youngest daughter was going to make the same mistakes her sister had. And although he knew how poorly he had handled Susan's pregnancy, he found himself fighting the same feelings of anger and resentment every time Sandra's boyfriend Craig came to pick her up. He knew he was being irrational, but he couldn't stand it any longer. When she woke up the next morning he was waiting for her. "Sandra, you are never to see Craig again. I can't trust you with him. That is my final word!"

■   ■   ■

About five years ago, when I was the youth pastor at a church in western Michigan, one of the television networks was running a story about teenagers and drugs. The next morning I had an appointment with a student at his school and was late getting into the office. I had five telephone messages on my desk, all of them from parents, all of them marked urgent, all of them about the special on TV the night before. I picked up the phone and dialed Jan. Her teenage son was one of my favorite students. Derrick was bright, articulate, funny, and serious about God. Jan was distraught on the other end of the phone. "Jack, did you see the special on TV last night? It was about teenagers and drugs. They gave the warning signs for parents and, Jack, I think Derrick is using drugs!"

I was more than a little bewildered at this announcement. I was quite sure that Derrick wasn't using drugs. As a matter of fact, Derrick didn't like to party at all. "Jan, what makes you think that Derrick is on drugs?"

"Well, on the show last night they gave some of the symptoms that parents should be aware of. One of them was sudden mood swings. And you know Derrick; he's very moody."

She was right. Derrick was moody. But mood swings aren't just a symptom of substance abuse. They are also symptoms of a pretty common ailment known as adolescence. I mentioned that to Jan, but fear had its grip on her now and she wasn't going to be assuaged by my words.

"Jack, they also talked about isolation. About kids who spend too much time in their rooms and are uncommunicative with their parents. Derrick comes home from school. I ask him how his day was. He says it was okay and then goes into his room. I need your help. I've already searched his room, and I couldn't find any drugs or anything associated with drugs. But I know he's hiding them somewhere!"

I stopped and thought for a moment. I knew when Derrick got home he and his mom were going to have a fun time trying to figure out the rights and wrongs of tearing apart his room, which he regarded as his private domain. I spoke a few empty words of encouragement to Jan, urged her not to go overboard, and hung up the phone, fully aware that a good mother-son relationship was about to be crashed on the rocks of irrational, dominating fear.

■ ■ ■

Patrick walked into his counselor's office demanding to see him. The secretary was close behind. "I told him you were busy, but he won't wait."

"That's all right, Jeanine. Patrick, your appointment isn't

until next week. What is so urgent that it can't wait a few days?"

"Alex, I don't know what to do. I know my wife is leaving me. I know she is having an affair. I can't sleep. I can't eat. I don't know what to do. She is out of town on business now, and I'm so afraid that she is cheating on me. I can't prove it, but I know it deep down in my heart."

Patrick's fear was eating him alive. He found himself quizzing his wife about every move she made, demanding to know why she had to travel so much or work late once in a while.

The next week Alex saw Patrick again. "I was right. She came home saying she couldn't take it anymore, that I was too crazy about her job and that she was leaving. You were wrong, Mr. Know-It-All Psychologist. She *was* going to leave me. I was right. But now, what am I supposed to do?"

■   ■   ■

Ken and Eleanor's daughter was crying. "But Mom, I'm twelve years old. All of my friends from church are going to camp. Why won't you let me go?" Eleanor looked at her husband.

He looked sternly at his oldest daughter. "We love you, that's why. Can't you get it through your head that we only want what's best for you? You're not old enough to go to church camp. We can't protect you there. Who knows what might happen without us to take care of you? You've never even been overnight alone without us. Five days at camp? No way!"

Eleanor listened to her husband and wondered if they were doing the right thing. They had kept a pretty tight leash on Lynnae. Her other friends had been going to each other's houses to spend the night, but Lynnae wasn't allowed to. After all, who knew what kind of television shows and movies she might be exposed to when she was out of their sight? Eleanor knew that most of her friends thought she and Ken were too hard on Lynnae and too overprotective. But when she thought of their daughter out there in the world, she got all tight inside, knowing all the ways that her daughter could fall into sin or be exposed to anti-Christian media. *We are right,* she thought, steeling herself inwardly for another tantrum from Lynnae. *We are protecting our daughter from the harmful influences of the world. No one can fault us for that. We are doing what God would have us do.* "Lynnae, I've heard enough. Go to your room. This discussion is over."

Late that night as they lay in bed, Ken and Eleanor talked about Lynnae. She was becoming more and more resentful of their tight grip on her life. But there was so much in the world to be afraid of. How could a twelve-year-old girl possibly know what was right and wrong? How could she make her own decisions?

■　　■　　■

Neal and Jill walked to their car slowly, their lips trembling with emotion. It wasn't supposed to be this way. Jill, seven months pregnant, was going in for an ultrasound. "It's probably nothing," they said. "Just routine because we want to be sure." Then, "We would like to do an amniocentesis. Just to rule some stuff out. Don't worry. It is not a problem." Now this, "Your son isn't developing as he should. We can't be positive but we think he has. . . ." They weren't even listening to the unpronounceable name that now defined their unborn son. They were in shock.

Now in the car, Neal and Jill let go, crying, holding each other, trying to still the fear that has gripped them. *How can we parent this boy? Will we make it? What are we going to do?* This pregnancy had been an answer to prayer. After years of trying, they were finally going to have the child of their dreams. People had asked, "What do you want? A boy or a girl?" They had smiled at each other and said in practiced unison, "We don't care, as long as it is healthy." How simple a request that seemed! Now this news, shaking them to their foundations. Praying late at night with his wife sleeping uneasily beside him, Neal cried out to God, "How am I going to handle this? Why are You doing this to us? I am so afraid. Please help me."

■　　　■　　　■

The insistent ringing of the phone woke Elizabeth up from a dead sleep. "Yes, this is Elizabeth Brown. Yes, he is my son. He's WHAT? In jail? I don't understand. Yes, I'll come right down. Thanks for calling."

Hurriedly, Elizabeth pulled on her coat, ran to the car, and drove to the police station. There she found her son Mike, drunk and snoring in a cell. He had vomited in his sleep, and the smell was overpowering. "Lady, do you want to take him home, or do you want to leave him here? Bail is $500."

"I don't know. I can't handle him anymore. He's nineteen. I can't keep rescuing him. I just don't know what I should do!"

Crying herself to sleep after bringing home her only son, Elizabeth wondered where she had gone wrong. How had this happened to her? This was the fourth time in three months that Mike had been involved with the police. Twice she had been hauled out of bed by sympathetic police officers who knew her. Her son seemed to be spinning out of control, and there was nothing that she could do about it. A gnawing fear gripped her heart. *I've failed as a parent,* she thought to herself as sleep refused to come. *It's my fault. If he doesn't turn out right, it will be because of me. If only his father hadn't left, if only I could have held the family together. I should have been a better wife, then he wouldn't have needed that young girl. I should have made my husband happy. I could have done so much more for him. I shouldn't have let him leave. But I failed, he left, and now my son is paying the price.*

■　　　■　　　■

The cynical psychologist left his office with tears in his eyes. He had seen it all a thousand times he thought, but today he had been touched in way he hadn't been touched in a long time. Counseling a family that was in the throes of a messy divorce, he had asked a seven-year-old child to draw a picture describing his family. The boy had resolutely gone to work and following almost a half an hour of intense labor had tentatively presented his picture to the therapist. He looked, swallowed hard, and showed the picture to the divorcing parents. They began to cry softly. The father got up and walked out with tears streaming down his face. The picture was of a grown man, standing at the door with tears running down his face. The little boy looked at his mother, "I'm just so afraid that Daddy isn't ever coming back."

"I know, Honey. I'm afraid too."

The talk afterwards was subdued. The questions simply: *Is this divorce going to wreck our son? Will he make it? Will our actions damage him permanently?*

■　　　■　　　■

My dad and mom were afraid too. My brother suffered from severe asthma and at two years old they had to rush him to the hospital because he wasn't breathing. Jon spent a week in an oxygen tent. Every night as Mom left him, he would cry and ask for a kiss through the plastic of the oxygen tent. My mom would cry all the way home, wondering if Jon would make it through the night, wondering if he would still be there in the morning. She wondered if this was to be the story of the rest of his life. A hospital existence. No one knew what would come of Jon's condition, whether his breathing problems would go away with age or get worse.

Every night of that long, hard week, without being able to touch or hold him, fear gripped my parents. Fear that their son would be taken from them, fear that he wouldn't be able to live a "normal" life like other little boys. And that fear was a cold claw on their hearts.

Ever since I can remember, my mom has been unable to go on a trip or to take leave of her children—and now her grandchildren—without saying good-bye. "Just in case," she says, "just in case I don't ever see you again." I asked her why she was so afraid of us dying or of not seeing us again, and she told me the story of how her father had gone into the hospital for routine surgery when she was only five years old. He had died in surgery. She was never able to say good-bye to him. She told me how since that time her fear of losing her family members had not diminished. Even though my brother's problems faded with age, her fear of losing us has not. It still haunts her in the night.

■   ■   ■

I looked at my daughter in her sleep last night, so beautiful, so bright, and so independent—only in the first grade and already nothing goes unchallenged. Erin wants to know why and how, and feels the injustice sorely when I reply with an impatient, "Because I told you so, that's why." I often wonder if she is going to turn out all right. I know she's smart. I know she'll grow up loved, but will she make good choices when she gets to high school? Will she find the right man to love? Will she become a follower of Jesus? I go to bed almost every night with a small cold fear lurking in the back of my mind for my oldest daughter.

■   ■   ■

Paul and Ruth worried too. They worried about their middle son. He seemed so withdrawn during his senior year of high school. He didn't say much to them, and now as he was preparing to leave for a large state university in California, they were even more worried. What would influence their son? Would he hang on to his faith? What about the values they had tried so hard to teach him? Would they be left behind when he "grew up" without them at college? On the night before Brian was to leave, Paul and Ruth prayed together, something they didn't do often. But both of them had been

18

unable to sleep. They were too afraid and needed to ask God to watch over their son. As they drifted into sleep, the "what if" questions held on relentlessly. They did not sleep well.

■   ■   ■

What do these very different families have in common? What is the thread that runs through their disparate stories? What binds them together? Only this: every one of these families, including my own, has been profoundly and powerfully influenced by fear. The family fears that these families illustrate changed the way they related to each other, caused them to say and do things they didn't want to and wished they could take back. Every one of these families was gripped by one of what we call *family fears*. When we look inside ourselves, we can see how our own family fears are often the hidden source of that anger that seems to come from nowhere. Being honest with ourselves, we see how our actions are many times influenced by our fears. Uncovering our defenses, we realize that too many times as parents, we allow the fear to speak and discipline.

What Is Fear?

Fear can be defined quite simply as an "emotional reaction characterized by unpleasant, often intense feelings, and by a desire to flee or hide." Most of us can identify with the description of unpleasant and intense feelings. And who hasn't felt the urge to run and hide when we are faced with fear-inducing situations? But just to define fear isn't enough. We need to take a closer look at the components of fear. It has three separate parts.

Cognitive: The first component of fear is the cognitive. The mind sends a message in reaction to an outside stimulus. This stimulus could be an out-of-control car when we are driving down a busy highway or the sight of one of our children heading toward the edge of the road. Our brain sends the message that something bad is about to take place. Truly and simply, fear begins in the brain.

Emotional: This message from the brain results in a feeling of anxiety, either acute as in the case of real immediate danger, or a general sense of anxiety that many of us feel every day. This feeling doesn't come from nothing. It is the direct result of a brain message. It is our emotions responding to the stimuli.

Physiological: The final component, the physiological, is the one that we associate most readily with fear. The sudden tightness in our stomachs when we descend the first hill of the roller coaster or the shortness of breath upon hearing bad news is the result of the cognitive and the emotional messages. In a way, the body is the last to get the news. This physiological aspect of fear can be very complex. Sometimes fear literally makes us sick; sometimes it produces a rush of adrenaline that causes us to react quickly to stimuli and avoid injury.

God created each of us with a sense of fear, and fear is often a useful, even needed, stimulus in our lives. Joseph Wolpe, one of the seminal thinkers on fear and behavior, writes:

> Fears may be considered useful when they are aroused in circumstances where there is a real threat; useless fears are aroused when there is no such threat. The contrast is illustrated by the following example. If, walking through a park, I come upon a snarling tiger, the fear I feel is appropriate because there is real danger. But if instead of a tiger, I see a small mouse and am terrified by that harmless creature, the fear is useless (*Our Useless Fears,* Houghton Mifflin, 1981, p. 7).

This book is about how we turn our mice into tigers, how we actually allow our family fears to grow until they really do terrify us and often control our lives. It is about useless fears that have become or are becoming reality. In *Family Fears* you will learn how the emotional, cognitive, and physiological components of fear can coalesce around your genuine concerns about your family and become family fears.

What are these fears that haunt us? Am I alone in feeling this way? Is there any hope for me? Why can't I live with my fears? What will my fears do to my family? How can I get past this fear? Does God care about my fear? Where can I go for help?

Many times fear is the unknown motivator in families, causing tension, disagreement, and difficult relations, and hatching countless arguments. It is an unseen but powerful force moving through family dynamics. It wreaks havoc on families, bringing some of them to their knees in despair. In thirty-three years of ministry to families, my father Jerry and I have watched fear rise up and ruin otherwise strong families. We have seen how devastating irrational, unchecked fear can be. We have listened to those who have been hurt and wounded by others' fears.

This book is about those family fears, about the fear that gnaws at parents late at night when their children haven't yet returned home. It is the fear a father feels when he watches his daughter grow up and turn into a woman. It is the often nameless anxiety that won't go away. In the next pages we will illustrate five common family fears. We will show how each fear can bring enormous stress into family relationships, change personalities profoundly, and ultimately dominate family dynamics. We will also show that there is hope, and there is help. Fear doesn't have to run our lives. There is a better way.

Family Fears

What Do I Worry About?

Complete the following self-test as honestly as you can. Answer the questions according to this scale:

SA - Strongly Agree
A - Agree
U - Undecided
D - Disagree
SD - Strongly disagree

I AM CONCERNED . . .	SA	A	U	D	SD
1. About how well my children are doing in school.	___	___	___	___	___
2. About my children's friends.	___	___	___	___	___
3. That my children will make bad decisions regarding sex, drugs, or alcohol.	___	___	___	___	___
4. About how well I am doing as a parent.	___	___	___	___	___
5. About how my children respond to peer pressure.	___	___	___	___	___
6. That my children are not well liked by their friends.	___	___	___	___	___
7. That my children will not "turn out right."	___	___	___	___	___
8. That we will have enough money for college for our kids.	___	___	___	___	___
9. That we fight too much as a family.	___	___	___	___	___

I AM CONCERNED . . .	SA	A	U	D	SD
10. That our marriage troubles will hurt my kids.	⎯	⎯	⎯	⎯	⎯
11. That my children will not continue in "the faith."	⎯	⎯	⎯	⎯	⎯
12. That my children will have an accident and get seriously hurt.	⎯	⎯	⎯	⎯	⎯
13. That my child will marry the wrong person.	⎯	⎯	⎯	⎯	⎯
14. That my children will not adopt my values as their own.	⎯	⎯	⎯	⎯	⎯
15. That my children's behavior will cause disrespect to our family name.	⎯	⎯	⎯	⎯	⎯

Add up all of your Strongly Agrees and Agrees. Assign each Strongly Agree 5 points, and each Agree 3 points. Enter your total score here:

⎯⎯⎯⎯

Remember this is not a complete psychological profile. The purpose of this test is to help you identify the areas in which you struggle with fear.

If you scored:
45+   . . . Fear is a dominant factor in your family life
30–44 . . . You are strongly influenced by fear
15–29 . . . Fear is influencing your family more than you realize
0–14 . . . Your fears are under control

CHAPTER TWO

The Cycle of Fear

What motivates us as parents? Certainly I am motivated by my love for my children. My love for them causes me to discipline them, to hug them, to want to kiss away all of their hurts and pains. I am also motivated by responsibility. I feel responsibility for my family. I feel a strong responsibility to nurture them, to provide for them, and to protect them as much as I can. Responsibility influences many of my decisions and actions.

There are, of course, many other motivating factors in my relationship with my children, including one that we don't talk about very often—a motivating factor that at times we are not even aware of, or if we do become aware of it, we push it deep down, trying to pretend it isn't there or that it doesn't really matter.

I'm talking about fear. It is our contention in this book that one of the profound and powerful motivating forces in families is fear. As a matter of fact, we believe that nearly all families are influenced by their family fears, some to a small degree, some a great deal. And that is all right, except that often we refuse to see our actions as the results of our fears. We deny that fear is influencing us, while its grip grows tighter around us. Christian counselor Norm Wright describes the motivating forces in our lives in his book *Uncovering Your Hidden Fears:*

> There are two great motivating forces in life: fear and hope. Interestingly, both of these motivators can produce the same results. Fear is a powerful *negative* drive. It compels us forward while inhibiting our progress at the same time. Fear is like a noose that slowly tightens around your neck if you move in the wrong direction. Fear restricts your abilities and thoughts and leads you to panic reactions. Even when you are standing on the threshold of success, your most creative and inventive plans can be sabotaged by fear (Tyndale House, 1989, p. 26).

The problem with fears, the reason we need so desperately to take a hard, honest look inside and identify them, is because of what uncontrolled, unrecognized, and unnamed fear can do to us. It is much more powerful than we care to admit, more controlling of our actions and our attitudes than we would like to believe. For many families the noose of fear is tightening around their necks. They are responding with panic, and in their urgent need to assuage their growing fears, they are feeding them, helping them take control of their lives. In our years of working with families from all over America, we have seen what fear can do to families. We have seen fear grab control and rip them apart. We have seen fear work quietly behind the scenes, sowing mistrust and suspicion. We have seen it rise up in anger, even violence.

Our fear affects us in many ways. It affects us psychologically, preying on our minds. It affects us emotionally, creating anger and distrust. Fear affects us physiologically, making us sick. Fear affects us relationally, changing the way we interact with others. And fear affects us spiritually, destroying peace and bringing pain into our souls.

Ultimately, *fear turns us inside out.* One father said it very well: "When my fear is in control, I become everything I hate.

And yet, I can't seem to stop. My fears are ruining my marriage and my relationship with my kids. I don't know what to do!"

Why should we take the trouble to look inside and identify our fears? Why should we have to worry about one more so-called family dysfunction? Because fear isn't just another "dysfunction." Fear causes dysfunction. Fear is a root cause and not just a symptom of a deeper problem. And fear can dominate our lives.

Five Reasons Why We Need to Identify Our Family Fears

1. Fear paralyzes us.

It makes us too cautious, afraid to make any decisions, fearing that we won't make the right one. Fear paralyzes us by robbing us of our self-esteem and stripping us of our confidence. One young mother was so afraid that she was disciplining her child poorly, she gave up trying to discipline at all. Of course now she is afraid that by not disciplining she is failing as well. Fear causes us to lie to ourselves, to pretend that bad things aren't going to happen in our family, and prevents us from taking the necessary preventative steps to keep those fears from becoming reality.

Chuck and Cindy were a well-respected, wealthy, prominent couple in their church. Chuck served as an elder; Cindy headed children's church. They had two beautiful teenage daughters, the perfect family. At least that is what they told everyone and that is the picture that everyone had of them. The truth was that their oldest daughter was sexually promiscuous and using drugs. She was wrecking her life, and they refused to consider the truth. They denied it. Why? Because they were bad parents? No. Because they didn't love their kids? NO. Because deep inside they were afraid that their daughter was going to break up the perfect picture. And by confronting her about her drug use and sexual choices, they would have had to confront their fears. Instead their fear paralyzed them. The tragedy is that they lost their daughter because of their fear of losing their daughter.

Paralyzing fear keeps us from making important decisions. We don't talk to our kids about their sexuality because we are afraid. We don't talk with our husbands or wives about tensions in relationships because we are afraid. We don't confront abusive backgrounds and parents because we are afraid. Instead we plod along with our eyes closed, hoping the worst won't happen if we just don't think about it. We think that if we talk about it or bring it up, even for a moment, we are going to bring it to pass. We become paralyzed, and ultimately this brings our worst fears into reality.

Are you afraid of your children's budding sexuality? I must admit that I am. I looked at my oldest daughter last week and fear coursed through my veins. Her mouth was changing. She was getting lips. I don't mean that she had a lipless face before, but her lips just kind of grew into big, full, almost grownup, going-to-be-beautiful-and-kissable lips. I'm looking ahead to her teenage years, and I'm scared to death. Some boy is going to kiss those lips! I'm not exaggerating when I tell you that the thought turns my stomach. I'm also not exaggerating when I tell you that talking about her budding sexuality isn't the easiest thing for me. But I do it because my worst fear is that she will make terrible sexual choices. In order to avoid that, I have to face my fear. My tendency is to bury my head and hope that she makes it without my instruction. My fear tells me not to bring it up, to just kind of hold my breath. But if I give in to my fear then I almost guarantee that my fears will be given credence.

2. Fear causes us to deny the providence of God.

Our fears deny God His role as the creator and sustainer of the universe. Our God tells us that He knows us so well that even the hairs on our heads are numbered. When our family fears are in charge, we are telling God that He isn't big enough, or that He doesn't care enough about our problems to handle them. We make a mockery of His promises to never leave us or forsake us. We forget about His hand on our lives. All that seems to matter is running from the fear inside. God seems far away and unconcerned. Fear causes us to become like Job, to look at God and accuse Him of letting the world spin out of control.

We are not suggesting that it is wrong or evil to question God, wondering why He allows bad things to happen to our families. We are speaking of the way our fears can kill our faith. Bernice is a Christian woman in her forties. Her life has not been easy, but through the difficult times she has learned to rely on God, knowing that He cared about her and would take care of her. Now, however, she is experiencing serious difficulty in her marriage. She lays in bed at night and wonders if God even cares. She is afraid that her husband is going to leave her, and her fear is driving the peace that comes from God completely out of her life. She has stopped talking with God and reading His Word. Her fear is gaining in strength even as her faith ebbs.

3. Fear causes us to become controlling people.

As we feel things moving beyond our grasp, as we deny God's providence, we set ourselves up in His place. We try to take control. We believe that if we can just keep a lid on everything, then nothing bad will happen. So we try to control our wives or our husbands. We insist that we need to know their every thought and action. They must account for every minute of every day. We try to control our teenage children. Don't go to movies; don't hang around those kinds of kids. Don't go out on a date; don't even go out of the house. We are trying to throw our arms around the world and gather it in. We are sitting in God's seat. Our fear is turning us into controlling people — difficult, unhappy, ultimately friendless people.

This attempt to control resembles the juggling circus clown. He starts juggling two bowling pins, then another clown tosses him a third, then a fourth. Soon the poor clown is desperately trying to keep six or seven pins from falling to the ground. Ultimately he misses one, and all of them come crashing down. Like the circus clown, we are trying to juggle too many things when we attempt to control our every circumstance. We can't do it, and sooner or later everything will come crashing to the ground. We cannot control others, not forever, not consistently. They will slip through our fingers.

4. Our fear causes anger.

As we lose control and things begin to slip through our fingers, we become angry. Your kids rent a video you had hoped to shield them from. Behind your back, your daughter goes out on a date with the wrong kind of guy. Your spouse resents your controlling attitude and distances herself. We say to ourselves, "I'm just trying to do what is right for them. Can't they see that?" Our fear lights the kindling wood of anger, and soon our concerns about family problems are real enough.

Glen and Joann are sitting uncomfortably in the counselor's office. They are uncomfortable because there is only one chair and one couch, and their counselor has claimed the chair. By default they must share a couch, and they aren't happy about it. You can feel the seething anger in the air between them. This is not their first session with this counselor. He is trying to find out the root of this anger that is killing their marriage.

As he talks to them, he realizes that Glen has a deep-seated fear that Joann is going to have an affair and leave him. To keep this from happening, Glen has attempted to keep Joann from any meaningful contact with other men. Every time she brings up a conversation she has had with a male coworker, he goes crazy and accuses her of an affair. After about five years Joann has had enough. She is angry with her husband for not trusting her, angry with him for trying to control her, angry with him for not giving her the benefit of the doubt. Glen is angry with Joann for defying him by continuing to have male friends. He is angry because she refuses to submit to him and follow his directions. Together they are one of the angriest couples their counselor had ever met. At first their counselor thought he saw their problem clearly. They were angry with each other. Resolve the anger—save the marriage. But after many hours with them he began to revise his estimate. The root problem was not the anger, but the fear. Fear was precipitating the anger. Anger was a symptom; fear was the problem.

5. *Fear urges us to run away.*

When our fears begin to take control we have two options—either fight or flight. When we choose to fight, we often become controlling. But many of us choose instead to run away and not face the consequences. Fear turns us into cowards. For some of us, fear causes us to leave our wives or to emotionally abandon our children when they enter adolescence. Our fear causes us to hold back our love or to refrain from vulnerability. In one instance a husband was afraid that his wife was losing interest in him. His fear caused him to withdraw from her emotionally. He was running from the confrontation he feared would come, running from the rejection he feared. As his wife felt him move away from her in an emotional sense, she became afraid that he was preparing to leave her, that he was having an affair, because he was so distant. By the time they came into the counselor's office, the mistrust and suspicion had grown so deep that they were legally separated. Their fear had caused them to run away.

Fear often functions as the catalyst of a chain reaction. Family fears can be the first domino that starts them all falling. Diagrammed, the cycle might look like the chart on page 32.

The "Fight" Cycle

As mentioned earlier, when fear begins to take control, we have basically two choices; either we try to fight it by controlling our world or we run away from it. Taking a look at the diagram again, we can follow the destructive cycle that con-

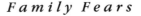

Fear Produces Two Resonses:
Fight and Flight

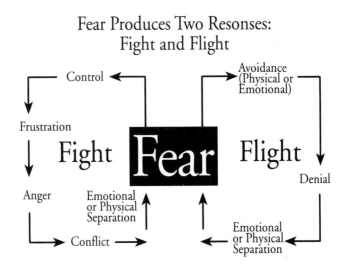

trolling fear often sets in motion by reading the story of Marie and watching the dominoes fall in her life.

The first link: control

Marie is afraid that her only son is hanging around with the wrong type of friends. She is worried that he is using drugs and drinking too much. Her fear — that he will let drugs and alcohol ruin his life — is a valid one and has become a powerful force in their family. But because she is afraid, Marie tries to control her son's every waking moment. She drives him to school and picks him up. When he goes out, she demands that he call in every two to three hours. She checks up on him by calling places that he said he would be. She tries to control him as much as possible. The problem, of course, is that no one can really ever control another human being if that other person doesn't want to be controlled. Jim resents his mother's overprotective control. It is stifling him, and he spends almost all of his waking hours trying to get away from her. He lies to her about where he is going, refuses to call and check in, and repeatedly violates his curfew.

The second link: frustration

Marie becomes frustrated because the tighter she tries to hold on, the more Jim slips through her fingers. The more control she tries to impose on Jim, the more he fights for freedom. Her inability to force him to follow her directions is birthing tremendous frustration. But she is not the only person frustrated. Jim feels completely frustrated as well. He is frustrated because he feels like his mom mistrusts him and treats him like a small child. This causes him to fight every new demand with all of his strength. Marie sees her fear of his rebellion coming true and tightens the screws. He just becomes more difficult to handle, and her frustration grows with each passing day.

The third link: anger

Inevitably that frustration on both of their parts becomes anger. And that's when they came to see me. "Because they were just so angry at each other." Psychologists call this the presenting problem. The presenting problem was that Marie was angry at Jim, (and her husband as well for not backing her up more enthusiastically), and Jim was angry at his mother because he perceived (correctly) that she was trying to run his life. Marie's anger moved her to try to achieve more control which started more frustration and inevitably added to the already considerable anger in the family. With each heavy-handed attempt at control, Jim grew angrier and withdrew further from his mother.

The fourth link: conflict

Marie's and Jim's anger spilled out of both of them into open war in their house. This conflict had become so painful that they could barely stand to be in the same room with each other. Eventually it seemed that everything became grounds for a fight. Every slight was reacted to defensively and self-

33

protectively, starting more conflict. Marie and Jim were deep into a cycle of destructive relating that had been started with fear. Now, of course, the fear was almost forgotten, buried under all the anger, frustration, and fighting, but it was still exerting its influence on Marie. With each fight and each hateful word, Marie's fears intensified. She was no longer just afraid that her son was going to abuse drugs or alcohol. She was now afraid that he was going to run away, that he would hate her forever, that she had bitterly failed as a mother.

Out of the conflict and ever-growing fear came intense pain. Every family member was hurt by the conflict, the tension, and the defensiveness. But this pain didn't drive Jim and Marie toward reconciliation. Instead it helped feed additional fears — fears that they would be hurt again, that this pain would become worse. Those fears hardened into a self-protective determination not to be hurt again, thereby starting the cycle all over again.

Jim and Marie illustrate the cycle of destruction that is set into motion by our fear. Marie's fears were legitimate. It is not wrong for her to worry to about her son's involvement in drugs and alcohol. It is normal to be afraid that he will become involved with the wrong kind of friends. But too often we move from fear to control, and attempts to control other people are doomed to failure. We can try to stave off our hidden fears by controlling our husbands, wives, or children, but eventually and inevitably they will escape our control. As a matter of fact, the more we try to control them, the more they will struggle to escape our net. This adds to our fears and provides a rationale for pulling the net a little tighter.

As our spouses or our children wriggle through our controlling hands, we become intensely frustrated. We begin to take responsibility for their actions, and then when they do not do what we want them to do, we are almost overwhelmed with frustration.

This frustration is inescapable. Unreasonable attempts at control will always end in frustration. One of the most important things that we must learn is that we cannot really make anyone do what they don't want to do. The old story is told of the three-year-old boy who took a cookie when his mother had expressly told him not to. His mother told him to go sit in the corner. He refused. She raised her voice slightly, and again told him to sit down.

The little boy said "NO" in no uncertain terms.

Angry now, her tone grew cold and menacing. "If you don't sit down right now, you are going to be in big trouble!"

Still the little guy resolutely took his mother on. "NO."

Mom was tired of this game. She picked up her son, carried him to the corner, and forcibly sat him on the chair. "You're sitting down now," she declared to him triumphantly.

Defiantly he looked at her and said, "I'm sitting down on the outside, but I'm still standing up on the inside!"

Our attempts to control often result in spouses or children sitting down on the outside but standing up on the inside. This again causes frustration.

This frustration easily and quickly slides into anger, which erupts into conflict, hurtful words and deeds, which in turn birth greater fears, and on and on the cycle goes.

The "Flight" Cycle

The other reaction to fear that many of us choose is running away. This sets another, equally painful cycle into motion. Sometimes our "flight" is a *literal, physical running away.* More often it is a refusal to allow ourselves to get hurt, an emotional withdrawal from a relationship or a friendship. This drawing away inevitably produces an emotional distance that translates into a physical or emotional separation. In other words, that which we are often trying to prevent, we bring about by running away.

Denial is another way that we take flight from our fears. It is easier to pretend that our fear doesn't exist, that we aren't really feeling this way, than to face our fears and handle them. What happens, though, is that our fears are still growing. They gnaw at us late at night when we can't sleep. Denial often leads to emotional separation and sometimes even to losing touch with reality. Believe it. We cannot run from our fears. They will follow us wherever we go. And with each step they grow hungrier and more powerful.

There is yet another option for us when we are controlled by fear — *the freeze option.* By freeze we mean that we ignore what is causing our fear, pretending that it doesn't exist. We are literally rooted to the ground because of our fear. We don't make any attempt to resolve the problem; we are too afraid even to run away. Cecil Osborne in his book *Release from Fear and Anxiety* writes, "In some instances this [option] can be fraught with great danger, particularly if the situation calls for flight and and the person is immobilized by fear" (Word, 1977).

Freezing is as troublesome a response as fight and flight because once again the root problems are never handled. Instead they grow and develop as we try our best to play ostrich and pretend they are not there. Be warned. Your fears will grow and multiply while your head is in the sand, and when circumstances finally force your head up you will be dismayed to see how they have grown.

The Pain Factor

Much of the fear in our lives is caused by a desire to avoid pain of any kind. Facing our fears carries a price of pain that we are often unwilling to allow. However, the pain of avoiding confrontation or the pain of trying to change our own actions is mild compared to the pain that results when we either run away or try to control others. Ultimately, the pain that comes from fear controlling us is much more devastating than the pain of handling that fear.

I hate to go to the dentist. I'm sure that many people feel the same way about that biannual visit as I do. As a matter of fact, when I got married and was out on my own, I decided not to go to the dentist any more. After all, every time I went to the dentist I came home in pain, and I even had to pay the man for the "privilege." I decided that as an adult, no one could tell me what to do. I was afraid of the dentist, afraid of the pain that inevitably accompanied each visit, so I stopped going. I didn't go for almost six years. But then something disturbing happened. One of my teeth started to hurt; I mean really ache. I ignored it for as long as I could and didn't tell my wife about it. I knew that Leslie would smile and make a dentist appointment, exactly what I was trying to avoid. So I tried to block it out of my mind. Finally, my head hurt so badly from my toothache that I could barely speak and even reading was painful. I broke down and told my wife. Leslie called the dentist. I reluctantly and fearfully went in, and patiently waited for the bad news. But I wasn't prepared for five cavities, two of them almost abscessed. The next two hours were an ordeal in survival as the dentist used every diabolical pain-inducing tool on his stainless steel, sterile tray to save my wayward mouth. I went home in a pain-induced, Novocain-covered stupor, and waited for Leslie to act Florence Nightingale to my wounded soldier. Nothing doing. "You were the one who refused to go to the dentist. You suffer the consequences." Ow! That hurt almost as badly as my mouth. Of course she was right. Too often we treat our fears like I treated my teeth. We try to ignore them and forget about them until they hurt so much that they drive us into cycles of destructive behavior that cause more pain than confronting them initially ever could.

It doesn't have to be this way. As we work with families, we see reasons for hope. We see families breaking the cycle of fear, growing into confident love and acceptance. It is not easy, and it is not an overnight process. Moving from fear to confident love is hard work. *Family Fears* was written to help get you going down the right path, to provide an impetus to break the cycle.

In the next five chapters we are going to discuss in detail the five major fears families face. We will look at what they are, why they are such powerful forces in families, and how they affect our family relationships. In these pages you will meet families just like yours and mine, families struggling to break through the cycle of fear, families trying to hold together through difficult times. Some of them will inspire you with their resourcefulness, some of them will shame you with their defeatism, but hopefully all of the families we become acquainted with will be instructive, serving as both good and bad examples.

The Five Fears of Families . . . An Overview

The first major family fear is the *fear that our children will make life-dominating mistakes.* This is the fear that haunts us when our teenagers are an hour past their curfews without a call. It is the icy cold that grips our hearts as we watch them leave our care and guidance as they depart for college. It is the stuff of sleepless nights and restless days. We wonder if they will make it into adulthood without really blowing it. It seems that today's world is so full of temptation and that there are so many ways and places to stumble. The news media fills our living rooms with images of rampaging, angry youths, seemingly in search of the next high or heist. One commentator aptly phrased our fears for children growing up at the end of the twentieth century when he said, "A schoolboy today faces more temptation on his way to school in the morning than Grandpa did on Saturday night when he went out looking for it." We fear that our children will stumble and make a mistake that haunts them for the rest of their lives.

The second major family fear is the *fear that our children will not "turn out right."* This fear deals with our children becoming adults. Will they ever amount to anything? Will they be successful in this increasingly competitive world? As Norm from the popular television sitcom "Cheers" once observed, "It's a dog-eat-dog world out there, and I'm wearing Milkbone underwear." Will our kids make it? Or will they settle for less than we had envisioned for them? Will they become human beings we are proud of? Kids we can point to with puffed out chests: "See that doctor? He's my son." Whatever it means to turn out right, and different families have different definitions of what that means, it is a profound worry for many families.

The *fear that we are failing as a family* is a growing force in families living at the end of the twentieth century. So many of the evils in this culture are blamed on poor families and bad parenting that we are often almost paralyzed trying to figure out what is the right way to parent. Are we too hard on our kids or too soft? Do we argue too much or maybe we don't argue enough and aren't expressing our true feelings? The publishing industry feeds those fears with every new "how-to-parent" book on the market. Is this fear haunting you? Do you lie to others about family devotions and prayer-time when they tell you they spend one hour a day in prayer with their kids (and you can barely find the time to say grace before the evening meal)? This fear can wreck a family as it searches for an unreachable goal, to be the perfect family, both spiritually and psychologically.

The fourth fear is a deep and abiding one for many of us. *We fear that a family member will die or be seriously injured or sick.* We all have friends or relatives who have lost a child, and when we think about it, we grab our children, hold them close, and wonder how we can protect them from the same fate. This fear courses down our spines, and of course we don't talk about it. After all, it seems silly to mention how death haunts us when we lie awake at night. It seems almost unchristian to admit that we are scared of losing our kids or having to walk down the road of cancer with a spouse. What happens when this fear becomes unmanageable? Can families survive this kind of pressure?

The last family fear that we will discuss in detail is the *fear that our children will not share our family's values and faith.* This fear is often awakened as we watch the children of our friends grow up, move away, and promptly forget everything that their parents taught them about right and wrong, good and evil. We wonder what will happen to our kids. Will they become serious Christians? Will God be a priority in their lives? Or will church and Christianity be cast off like ancient beliefs in the Easter Bunny and Santa Claus? This is a sore spot for me, cause for serious anxiety in my life, and, as you'll find out in chapter seven, a serious spot for worry for my long-suffering parents as well. This fear is valid and real, influencing our actions and reactions beyond what we acknowledge.

The Five Major Family Fears

Check the ones that apply to you:

- ☐ 1. I am afraid our children will make life-dominating mistakes.
- ☐ 2. I fear that our children will not turn out right.
- ☐ 3. I sometimes feel that we are failing as a family.
- ☐ 4. I often worry that a family member will die or suffer a serious accident or illness.
- ☐ 5. I am afraid that our children will not live out our family's values and faith.

These fears are more powerful in our lives than we care to admit. We must find ways to overcome them. In this book families will find the hope and help they need to effectively deal with their fears. But first, we need to know the characteristics of these fears. We need to see how they manifest themselves in family dynamics. The next pages of this book will intimately acquaint you with the five major family fears. Through the self-tests and checklists you will have an opportunity to see what your family fears are and how they are affecting your family.

PART TWO

The Five Family Fears

CHAPTER THREE

No Second Chances?

*The Fear That Our Children Will Make
a Life-Dominating Mistake*

Bill walked up the stairs slowly. It was late. Once again he had been unable too sleep and had spent the better part of the night flipping channels with the remote. The TV could neither lull him to sleep nor calm the worry that consumed him. Finally, at 4 A.M., he had had enough and started for bed. On his way he stopped at the door to his daughter's bedroom. The door was open a crack. He pushed it wider and looked in. Could it be that Lisa was already seventeen years old? It seemed like yesterday he had held her in his arms, spun her on the merry-go-round, kissed her hurts away. Sleeping, she was peaceful and beautiful — so different from her waking hours, when she was defiant, rebellious, and openly promiscuous. As Bill wearily climbed into his bed for a couple of restless hours of sleep, he wondered what had gone wrong. Why had she become so difficult?

He knew that it had been hard for Lisa since her mother had left. At first the divorce drew them together, but lately he had seen her changing. She was hanging around a completely different crowd. Her boyfriend was a high-school dropout who didn't exactly dress for success. Lisa had told Bill they were sleeping together. She threw it out as a kind of challenge, one he didn't know how to meet. Then came the calls from school.

"Lisa was drunk in class this morning." "Lisa has been suspended for skipping." "Lisa is failing history." It seemed that during the last few months, at every fork in the road, she had taken a wrong turn. With every choice between right and wrong, she had willingly chosen wrong.

Bill prayed desperately as he went to sleep, "Please, God, watch over her. She could make a mistake that will wreck her whole life, her future. Please watch over her."

■   ■   ■

Jamie's voice was hoarse on the phone. He had been crying. "Mom, I'm in jail. I was in a car accident coming home from the concert. I had been drinking a little, and I hit a car on the side of the road. I think. . . ." He started to cry, loud anguished sobs coming over the phone. "I think that I may have hurt someone real bad. He might die. . . ."

Jamie's mom and dad spent the long drive to the jail wondering what they were going to do. Jamie was a straight "A" student who hadn't ever been in trouble. As far as they knew, he had never had a drink of alcohol before. Now, with his college application to an Ivy League school accepted, headed for success, the class valedictorian, he was in jail pending charges of manslaughter. Where had they gone wrong? How could they have protected him from this? Had they failed as parents? What would his future hold? These questions hung in the car, deadening their spirits, poisoning the air.

■   ■   ■

These real-life stories may strike a chord with you. Many of us spend sleepless nights worrying that Lisa's or Jamie's story will be played out in our own homes. We worry that our children will make a mistake with far-reaching consequences. We hear of other children, raised by good parents, who get pregnant, use drugs, or run into trouble with the law. We see church kids, youth-group regulars, drink and drive and wonder if we don't know everything that our own children are doing.

This worry is the first major family fear: *the fear that our children will make a life-dominating mistake.* It is one of the most common and powerful fears influencing our families. Who hasn't looked at the epidemic of teen pregnancy and feared for their children? Who hasn't seen a television special on AIDS and wondered how to prevent their children from becoming sexually active? Who doesn't realize the damage alcohol can do to teenagers and feel powerless to help their kids stay away from it?

This fear is not irrational. America at the end of the twentieth century is filled with opportunities for our children to wreck their lives. We live in a sex-saturated, pleasure-seeking culture. The very things that we hope our kids don't get involved in are advertised relentlessly through the mass media. We have every right to be concerned. The problem begins when this concern becomes fear, and when the fear becomes the parent. Out of control, this fear can be as destructive to a family as a Midwestern tornado.

What Is the Fear of a Life-Dominating Mistake?

This fear has two parts. First of all, *it is a fear that our children will make bad decisions.* This fear is especially powerful for parents of adolescents. Our kids make a tremendous number of important choices during their teens and early twenties. It is natural that some of the decisions they make will not be good ones. They must choose their college, their friends, their career, their husband or wife. They must decide what they are going to believe and what value system they will embrace. And they must make hundreds of little choices every week. *Do I take that drink? Do I dare to drive that fast?* Many of these choices seem small, but any one of them could have far-reaching consequences.

This brings us to the second part of this fear. *We are afraid that the bad choices will have long-term or even permanent consequences.* That is why we fear our children's sexual choices so much. We can't go out on dates with them, but we wish we could. Sexual choices are so fraught with danger. These choices can literally be a matter of life and death. Many of us have made poor sexual choices ourselves and know the emotional price that we paid. So we worry, and that worry grows into full-blown fear.

We also worry about drugs and alcohol. One bad decision can change a life in an instant. Twenty years of the best plans and intentions can fall by the wayside in a split-second swerve and tumble of a car over an embankment following a celebratory, alcohol-filled night. We may recall with dismay the drug-induced death of Len Bias, first-round draft pick of the Boston Celtics, on the very night of his pick, at a celebration for him, the millionaire-to-be. That could be our kids.

So we fear. We fear that in a moment's time our kids lives can go down the drain. We fear they will make a life-dominating mistake. A mistake, a bad choice, a poor decision that they will have to live with for a long time.

Why Is This Fear So Powerful?

Though it often goes completely undetected or seems disguised as legitimate concern, the fear of life-dominating mistakes pulls the strings of most parents. This fear is powerful for at least four reasons.

First, this fear can dominate family dynamics because parents know *bad choices can affect the quality of their children's lives forever.* One father expressed this very plainly when he said, "If my daughter gets pregnant, it's good-bye college, good-bye good job, good-bye nice life. She'll be stuck. And everything her mother and I have tried to teach her will go down the drain."

That is why we are so afraid. We all know someone like Jamie, someone with the world by the tail, until one night, or one careless party. Then boom—the bottom drops out, and the child's quality of life goes down the tubes. (Or so we

46

think.) We want our kids to live the American dream. We want to see them enjoy high school, love college, and find a good mate. We want to see them make something of their lives, and we see these terrible pitfalls on the way to that dream life. As we watch their friends or other family members fall into the traps, we vow to keep our children from the same fate, and our fear grows by leaps and bounds.

Our worry, essentially, is that all the hard work of parenting and all of the good choices that our children have made will be undone in one moment, and that our children's lives will not be what we want them to be.

Our culture's view of the role of parents is that the parents' job is to prepare their children for a better life than they had. As parents we are viewed as successes or failures based largely on the success or failure of our children. And as parents we know that our children's quality of life is shaped at least in part by the choices they make when they are younger. So we worry, and the worry grows into fear, and the fear makes us try to control our children or makes us distance ourselves from them so as to distance ourselves from the possibility of failure. What we often fail to realize is that our children's future quality of life could just as easily be adversely affected by our fear-influenced actions.

The second reason these fears are so powerful is because *a life-dominating mistake can destroy our dreams for our children.* We have dreamed about our children's futures for years. We have their lives all mapped out in our heads. We have big plans for them, and a life-dominating mistake can cause all of those plans to unravel, all of those dreams to come to naught.

MaryAnne is a single mom. Her three children are good kids. They get good grades. They are home when they are supposed to be. They go to church and youth group. Since MaryAnne's divorce nine years ago, she has not been able to give her children all she wanted to give them. Finances have been tight. Her job brought in enough to pay for necessities, but there wasn't much left over for fun. Her dream is that her oldest daughter, Chris, a straight "A" student, will get a scholarship to a good university and will go on to medical school. It is a cherished dream, one that she nurtures as she spends her days working hard to make ends meet. She visualizes her daughter's graduation from medical school, her high-rise office, even the car her daughter will drive. And it all hinges on one thing: her daughter's grades.

But all is not well in MaryAnne's dream. Her daughter has started dating a guy who doesn't go to church, works in a convenience store, and has seemingly no ambition. MaryAnne's daughter has told her that they are in love and that as soon as she graduates from high school, they are going to be married. MaryAnne can't believe it. It seems like the end to all her dreams, all because of some foolish adolescent infatuation. So she blew her top. She really let her daughter have it. She didn't mean to, but the fear welled up inside of her so quickly and so strongly that it wouldn't be denied.

"I can't believe that you are going to throw your life away on that worthless piece of trash. After all I've sacrificed for you over the years, so you could have something better. Now this is the thanks I get! The next time you want to wreck your life, why don't you just jump off a cliff? Because that's what you're doing here!"

Chris had run from the room crying. MaryAnne heard the door slam as she ran sobbing from the house. *Great*, MaryAnne thought, *she's probably going over to see him right now.* Then the despair overwhelmed her, and she started to cry. Graduation was two months away. Would her daughter wake up to the truth in time, or would all of her dreams for a better life for Chris go down in flames? She didn't know the answer, and the fear that Chris was going to make a huge mistake was driving her crazy.

MaryAnne's story is often repeated in smaller ways in our own lives. We have dreams for our children, both big and small, and we know that one bad choice could cause those dreams to come tumbling down like a house of cards. Our dreams for our children are what keep us going as parents. We hope that when all is said and done, they will have something better than we had. A better education maybe, or a better job. Maybe a better marriage than ours which may have ended in shame and pain. Often our dreams for our children become the vindication for our entire lives. We haven't achieved what we so confidently set out to do, and we want our children to reach those goals for us. Because even if we don't get the big house on the hill and the Jaguar in the driveway, if our children do, then we have vicariously attained it. We live out our failed ambitions and goals through our children, and the fear that they also will fail to achieve what we failed to achieve surrounds us and causes us to drive our children on to the goal. And in the back of our minds, with a lifetime of experiences to prove it, we know that one false step, one bad move, and it could all be over. We realize that some of these goals are so fragile that one life-dominating mistake will render it impossible for our children to reach them. And we are afraid. We are afraid because it is one thing to fail ourselves, but another far worse thing to watch our children fall where we have fallen, fail where we have failed, and give up as we have given up.

This destruction of our dreams is not just limited to big things like choice of a mate or a career. Often through our limited perspective we think that little missteps on the road are the life-dominating mistakes that we fear so much. We confuse our big, important, substantive dreams with our inconsequential ones.

Frank is a great example of this. Frank always dreamed of making the winning basket at the state championship game. He knew that his time would come to shine on the basketball court and that his high school years would be crowned with athletic glory. Unfortunately, Frank and the coach didn't get along too well, and two thirds of the way through his senior season Frank was tossed off the team—a team that went on to lose in the district finals by two points. Now Frank's son is in high school, and Frank wants his son to have the success he dreamed of but never realized on the court. He has been grooming Frank Jr. since grade school to be a good basketball player, and all that hard work has paid off. His son is not just a good basketball player, but a great one. As a sophomore he led the team in scoring and assists. Major college scouts were starting to drop by his games and practices. Clearly Frank Howligan Jr. had a bright future.

How bright they didn't even realize until at one game there were scouts from the three previous NCAA championship teams in the stands for one of Frank Jr.'s games. And he didn't disappoint: 27 points, 10 assists, and 10 rebounds—a triple double! Frank Sr. could hardly contain his enthusiasm. His son was going to be covered in the athletic glory that had unfairly been denied him and was going to succeed beyond even his wildest dreams.

The next morning Frank Sr. received a call at work from his son's school. "Mr. Howligan, we are afraid that your son may have cheated on his history exam. He and two other members of the basketball team missed exactly the same questions and wrote exactly the same answers for the essay portion of the test. We have suspended him from the team until we can investigate this further and determine whether he did in fact cheat. I must tell you, Sir, that if we find he did cheat we will declare him ineligible for the rest of the season."

Hanging up the phone, Frank Sr. was sick to his stomach. How could his son have been so dumb? Didn't he know what he was jeopardizing? He could have ruined everything for a stupid grade on a history test. All of his dreams could turn to ashes. He was suddenly very angry, but even stronger than the anger was the fear, the fear that everything he had been living for would go down the drain because of one silly mistake.

You and I may look at Frank's story and wonder how he could attach so much importance to a basketball game. We think rightly that he is overreacting and that Frank Jr.'s life isn't really destroyed forever. But we all have our pet dreams for our children and to us they are of vital importance. When they are threatened, we react strongly, and the fear wells up within us.

Our dreams for our kids are important things. They have

been formed over years and nurtured in our minds. When they are threatened, we will react and react very strongly. Our fears will rise up and choke us, drowning out our reason and our better judgment. When our dreams are being destroyed, we will do almost anything to save them. That is why this fear, that our children will make a life-dominating mistake, is so powerful. Because the power of our dreams cannot be overestimated.

The third reason that this fear holds so much power over us is that *life-dominating mistakes often embarrass and shame our family.* When your daughter walks into church eight-months pregnant at age seventeen, everyone is going to know whose child she is. When your son's name makes the papers because of a run-in with the law, your family is embarrassed. This need to avoid family shame and embarrassment is particularly powerful in the lives of Christian families. For some reason, we believe that we aren't allowed to make the same mistakes as other people, that our kids' mistakes show us to be not only ineffectual parents but poor spiritual role models and bad Christians too.

Growing up in a minister's family, I heard this refrain all too often: "You can't do that, Jack. What would people think of your father?" Or even more menacing, "Jack, if you ever mess up like so-and-so, you'll wreck your father's ministry." When I think back to those times, I realize now that my mother was afraid I was going to make a life-dominating mistake. And given many of my actions as a teenager, that was not an unreasonable fear. That fear was made more powerful by the fact that my father was a prominent pastor and Christian educator, and my mom worried that my miscues would reflect badly on him. She was worried about the shame and embarrassment that I might bring to the family name. One humorous incident illustrates my mom's fear very well.

I was sixteen, newly licensed by the State of Michigan to drive an automobile. I had a girlfriend who lived about forty-five miles away, so naturally I was always asking to borrow the car to go see her. On the day after Thanksgiving, which also happened to be a day after a particularly nasty winter storm, I approached my father about borrowing our big Chevy for the trip to Karlene's house. I approached my father because I knew that with snow on the ground there was no way that my mom was going to let me go. Thankfully, Dad readily agreed. I hurriedly showered and shaved (although I certainly didn't need the latter) and made my way as quickly as I could toward the front door. The goal was to be gone before my mom realized what was happening and could stop me from going.

I was almost out the door. I had one foot in the snow and the door was swinging shut when I heard my mom's voice, "Jack, where are you going?" In our family it was pretty much a cardinal sin to ignore our parents, so with a grimace I swung around and informed my mom that I was going to Karlene's house and that Dad had given me permission.

My mom listened quietly, then said, "Well you're not going until I see what you are wearing." I looked at her and with more than a little irritation told her that she must be having trouble with her eyes as it was obvious that I was wearing jeans and a polo shirt. My mom looked at me kind of funny and said, "That's not what I wanted to know. I want to know what underwear you are wearing."

Well at this point I have to admit that I lost it. I thought that my mom had gone completely insane. After all, it isn't every day that a mother asks her sixteen-year-old son on his way to a date what underwear he is wearing. I told her I was wearing my favorite underwear. My mom told me that I wasn't allowed to leave the house until I put on some newer underwear. (My favorite underwear being stuff I had been wearing since about the fifth grade.) I refused to change and was starting to get pretty embarrassed by the whole discussion.

At this point my dad walked into the room and wondered what was going on. I told him that Mom wanted to check and see what underwear I was wearing. He looked at her quizzically, not quite understanding her point. She then uttered the immortal cliché, "There is no way that he is leaving this house wearing those underwear. What if he gets in an accident and has to go to the hospital? What will people think of me? I would be so embarrassed."

I was now completely exasperated. "I'm just sure, Mom, that I'll get into an accident and I can hear the ambulance driver now. 'Hey, Bud, let's get this poor kid to the hosp . . . Wait a minute! Look at this underwear. There is no way I'm taking this kid anywhere. What kind of mom would let her kid out in this stuff?' " With that little burst of sarcasm, I left the house and headed for my girlfriend's.

About halfway there it started to rain and I couldn't get the windshield wipers to work. So I looked down for a moment, a very bad decision as it turned out. For the moment I looked down the car in front of the car in front of me stopped. And the car in front of me stopped, and I also stopped, but not of my own volition. At about forty-five miles per hour I slammed into the car in front of me, pushed that car into the one in front of him, and slid out into the other lane of traffic where I was hit by a pickup truck. I spun around and ended up in the ditch, my head coming into rather sudden contact with the windshield. And as I sat in that ditch with my head throbbing, the wail of sirens in the distance, and gesticulating, angry drivers at my window, all I could think of was my mother, my underwear, and a sudden worry that she might be right!

Now what was really bothering my mother? It was fear. She was afraid of the shame and embarrassment that I might bring to our family. Of course it was all humorous and became a story we tell every time we talk about family fears. But for many families this is not a laughing matter. Their fear of shame or embarrassment caused by a child making a life-dominating mistake ruins their relationships with their children. As a youth minister and speaker, I have known girls who never told their parents they were pregnant; they just went out and had abortions. Why, I ask them? "Because my dad said if I ever brought shame into my family like that, he would throw me out, and I believe he would." I have seen kids afraid to call their parents with news that they had been caught drinking and driving. Not because their parents would discipline them, but because their parents had made it very clear that the worst sin they could commit was bringing dishonor to the family name. And they were legitimately fearful of being disowned.

The fact that a life-dominating mistake brings shame and embarrassment upon a family feeds that fear and makes it stronger. It is one of the truly powerful forces in our lives. As one father told his daughter, "It took us twenty years to build up this family's name in this town, and you could wreck it all in one night."

The fourth reason this fear holds so much sway over us is that *a life-dominating mistake can mean financial hardship,* certainly for the child involved, but also potentially for the entire family. Families already struggling to make ends meet do not need the added burden of medical bills from a pregnancy or accident. They can't handle the additional expense. One father told his daughter after she informed him that she was pregnant, "Honey, we can't support you and the baby. We are barely making it now. I don't know how we are going to pay for the hospital and doctor, not to mention clothes, formula, and everything else. It all costs money, and frankly we don't have it."

Why is the fear that our children are going to make life-dominating mistakes such a motivating force in family relationships? Because these mistakes affect the quality of our children's lives, usually long-term, sometimes forever. Because these mistakes can destroy our dreams, and our dreams are things that we will fight for, things that we will fear for. Because a life-dominating mistake can bring shame and embarrassment to our family. And because a life-dominating mistake can bring financial hardship.

How Does This Fear Affect Us?

The fear of a life-dominating mistake changes the way we relate to our children, shapes our family dynamic, influences our parenting style, and can become the dominant force in our families. This fear affects us all in at least three different ways:

1. It causes us to overreact and overprotect.
2. It limits experiences and personal growth.
3. It fosters dependence and discourages independence.

Ultimately this fear causes us to act in ways that actually bring our worst fears to pass.

Perhaps the thing that causes more damage in our families than anything else is the way we overreact and overprotect when this fear is in control. In the first chapter we told the story of the mother who was convinced her teenage son was on drugs because of his "mood swings" and how she had already torn his room apart in search of nonexistent evidence. That story continues.

After her son returned home from school, he walked into his bedroom, put his book bag on his bed, and immediately knew that someone had been searching his room. "Mom, were you looking through my room today?"

"Yes I was. It's still my house and if I want to look through your room, I will, anytime I feel like it. Besides I did it for your own good."

"What on earth were you looking for?"

"I was looking for drugs."

"Drugs? I don't take drugs! What is wrong with you? You break into my room and invade my privacy. You don't trust me. I can't believe you!"

"Don't talk to me like that, young man. I'm your mother, and I will do what's best for you."

"You are insane, Mom. I can't understand you. Don't ever go through my room without my permission again!"

"You can't talk to me like that. You're grounded for two weeks."

"That's not fair! You're being stupid."

"One month!"

"MOM!"

"Six weeks!"

This overreaction drives reason out of our parenting. We react viscerally and very strongly. We see any discussion or expression of outrage or injustice as a challenge to our authority. So we overreact again with an unfair or ill-thought-out punishment or with hurtful words of anger. Our overreaction escalates what may have started out as a minor problem into a much larger, more complex situation.

Consider the preceding story. This mother has a real problem now. She goaded her son into disrespect, then punished him for expressing his outrage. What she needs to do is apologize and lift the grounding, but she feels afraid and threatened. There is no way, with her fear in control, that she is going to be rational enough to say, "I'm sorry. I was afraid. I blew it. I should have trusted you." Instead, her son's strong reaction makes her feel more insecure, feeling that if he is so worried about her going through his room that he must have something to hide.

Overreaction, caused by fear that our children will make a life-dominating mistake, can drive a wedge into our family relationships. Husbands and wives accuse each other of not caring enough or of belittling their concerns. Kids feel mistreated, and a strong sense of injustice births lasting resentment. This pulls families apart, sometimes leading to the very thing that Mom or Dad was so fearful of in the first place — a life-dominating mistake.

Overprotection is nearly as dangerous as overreaction. We've talked about this earlier in the book, how we try to control every aspect of our children's lives and the complete impossibility of ever accomplishing that task. Our children will either rebel against our heavy hand or grow up unprepared for the decisions and complexities of a very gray world. But this fear is so powerful that overprotection seems like a logical response to the very real dangers we perceive. The need to have an eye on our children all the time, even into their later teens and early twenties, causes great tension in our relationships. But it doesn't matter, because we feel that we are the only ones who can keep them from trouble, steer them away from a disastrous choice. We need to feel that we are in control, that we are in charge.

Unfortunately, this is poison for our kids. They do not mature into the kind of people we want them to be when we set out on this course. They don't become leaders who do the right thing against all others. Instead, we create weak followers who merely trade us for some other authority figure later in life, be that a husband or wife, a boss or a university professor. Then we lose contact and wonder what happened to our beloved children. Our worst fears come true because of the harm we do trying to protect them from those very mistakes.

This fear also does harm by limiting experiences. We are afraid that something awful will happen, so we don't let our children do anything. They never grow because growth is largely a result of experience. They never get to experience the world in all of its wonder and richness, a world that God created and put His personal stamp on.

While growing up, I often vacationed in the Upper Peninsula of Michigan. It was then, and largely still is today, an untamed, unpopulated, beautiful wilderness. My dad would often take us hiking around majestic Tahquamenon Falls, which were set back into the woods and in those days reachable only by a long walk. We would hike around the falls, climbing rocks, jumping across crevasses. Our goal was to get close enough to feel the spray from the gigantic upper falls and actually walk around the much smaller lower falls. It was tremendous fun, but it scared my mother to death. She was worried that we would take a misstep and tumble into the swirling waters, never to be seen again. She talked to my dad about it, but he was adamant. "I want the kids to experience this, to see God's creation in all of its glory." My mother steeled herself and even joined in on some of our hikes.

I'm so glad that Mom didn't let her fear control her. Some of my best memories are of crawling around the rocks with my dad and brother. In a lot of ways I learned how to be a dad while hiking with my own father. I learned how to have fun, how to judge risk versus reward, and how to take responsibility for my own actions. After all, if I decided on a path that led me into a dead-end, or worse, into the river, it was up to me to get back out. The experience was necessary and valuable. If my mom would have refused to let us play and learn and grow on those rocks, we would not have had the experience to look back on and draw from.

In a very real way we are the products of our experiences. It is only by doing that we learn. Now I am not advocating that our children try drugs or alcohol just for the experience. But I *am* strongly suggesting that our fears often keep our children from really seeing the world around them. They are bystanders and this world is passing them by. God "richly provides us with everything for our enjoyment" (1 Timothy 6:17). We want our children to live and enjoy every moment for God, not watch the world like they watch television. They need to experience the joy and the pain of real life. Our fears can keep them from doing this.

The third thing that the fear of a life-dominating mistake does to our children is to *foster dependence.* We are so afraid that our kids are going to make a bad decision that we don't let them make any decisions at all. We would rather trust ourselves and our judgments. So we try to keep our kids under our thumb. We attempt to control everything that we can. Unfortunately this limits our children's growth. They never move far enough along the continuum from dependence to independence as they grow up. The story of Jo and her teenage boys is instructive in this regard.

Jo was a good mom who struggled with the fear that her children would make a life-dominating mistake. She was so afraid of outside influences on her children that she virtually sealed them off from the outside world. She home-schooled them, didn't allow them to date, and didn't own a television. Movies and rock music were out of the question. Jo believed that if she could control what went into her children's minds and control their environment that she could control them. And for a while it worked. They were perfect children who did her bidding, answered her questions correctly, and did not rebel. She knew that she had chosen the right course.

But when her children graduated from high school, they

showed no signs of going to college or moving out. She tried to encourage her oldest to go to an acceptable Christian college, but he wouldn't budge. He seemed paralyzed, unable to become an adult.

Jo fostered a tremendous dependence in her children. They were completely dependent on her and completely subject to her authority. She hoped to keep them from danger that way, to keep from making the same mistakes her friends' children were making. She wanted to make sure that they were successful and that nothing they did while young would destroy their lives. And to a large extent she succeeded. Except her children never moved into independence. They never learned how to make a decision. They never grew up. And now their quality of life is not good. They are in their late twenties and still at home, still working menial jobs, still children. Jo's fear drove her to control; her control made her worst fears come true.

One of the major developmental tasks in adolescence is to move from dependence/childhood to independence/adulthood. Our controlling actions, coming from our fear that our children will make a life-dominating mistake, foster dependence and kill independence. We may succeed in keeping our children from harm, but in making all their decisions for them we have also succeeded in keeping them children. This presents a problem, because we are forced to either kick them out of the nest or continue to keep them dependent on us. When we kick them out of the nest, they are usually not equipped to handle the real world in all of its complexity and ambiguity. Right and wrong are much harder in the real world than just doing what Mom and Dad say. There is a very real chance that our children, once finally on their own, will seek out someone else to depend on, someone who doesn't share our values or who doesn't have their best interest in mind. They may be led into the very behaviors we are terrified of.

The fear that our children will make a life-dominating mistake is a valid fear. The world is a scary place for parents who take the time to look around. It seems that every time I look up, things are getting worse. I worry for my three children. I fear that they will take that fatal misstep and ruin their lives. You probably look around your town and feel the same way. That's all right. It's okay to be afraid. Everything that we fear could actually happen. It is unlikely, but very possible.

How are you going to deal with your fear? How are you going to handle it? Will you let it control you, pushing you into overreaction, overprotection, and controlling, manipulative parenting? Or will you learn how to respond appropriately and biblically? In just a few chapters we'll talk about how to control our fears, how to handle them instead of letting them handle us. We'll talk about the steps we can take to bring them under control. Read on!

Chapter Checklist

Complete the following checklist and talk about it with your family. Use this scale to answer each statement. Circle the number which best represents your answer.

1 = Strongly Agree, 2 = Agree, 3 = Undecided,
4 = Disagree, 5 = Strongly Disagree

1 2 3 4 5   1. For the most part, my children make very good decisions.

1 2 3 4 5   2. I have great dreams for my children.

1 2 3 4 5   3. I don't worry much about my children's decisions embarrassing me or bringing shame to my family.

1 2 3 4 5   4. I encourage my children to think and act independently.

1 2 3 4 5   5. I encourage my children to try new things, even when there is the potential of failing.

1 2 3 4 5   6. I allow my children to fail.

1 2 3 4 5   7. I freely allow my child to choose his/her own friends.

1 2 3 4 5   8. I have great faith in my child's abilities to make the right choices when he/she has the opportunity to make bad choices.

1 2 3 4 5   9. A bad choice doesn't mean "the end of the world" for my child.

1 2 3 4 5   10. Sometimes our children need to learn the hard way.

Scoring: If you scored less than 25 you are not overly concerned about your child making bad choices that will alter his/her life permanently. A score between 25 and 35 indicates some uncertainty on your part regarding your child's choices. If you scored over 35, you may be overly concerned (fearful) about your child's choices.

CHAPTER FOUR

What Are You Going to Do with Your Life?

The Fear That Our Children Will Not "Turn Out Right"

Fred looked around uneasily at his Sunday School class. It was time for fellowship, a time when all the other fathers, or so it seemed, would drink coffee and brag about their children's latest accomplishments. Dan's son was finishing medical school; Andy's was already a neurosurgeon. And if Fred had to hear Cliff talk one more time about how much money his daughter was making at that advertising firm, he would just explode. Inevitably they would turn to Fred and inquire, "What about your kid, Fred? Whatever happened to your son? What is he doing anyway?" Then Fred would mumble something about "still finding his way" and try to laugh it off.

The truth was that he was worried. His oldest son had dropped out of college after only one semester, and not a good semester either. He had been working at the convenience store and hanging around home. Fred was very concerned that his son just wasn't turning out right, that he wasn't going to amount to much. What really scared him was thinking about how all of the money he had poured into Christian school and all the effort he had put into parenting might come to nothing. Walking out to his car, he suddenly looked at his wife.

"Honey, is Jeff all right? I mean, is he going to be all right? Or is he, a, well, a loser?"

Kate looked at Fred and smiled. "Come on, Fred. He's still young. He's got lots of time to grow up. Don't worry about it!"

"But I do worry about it. I think about it a lot. As a matter of fact, I can't stop thinking about it. I've got to do something to get him off his behind. He's not going to amount to anything."

Not long ago we were speaking on the subject of this book. After our talk, an attractive couple in their forties waited to speak with us. Their problem was stated simply and plainly: "Jack, our son is twenty-five and shows no sign of ever growing up. He is still living at home, still hangs around with his old high school friends. He is going to college part-time but not doing very well. We're just afraid that he's not going to turn out right."

I asked them what they meant by "turn out right." They replied that it meant doing better than they had, or at least doing as well as they had. It meant a good job, family, and responsibility. I asked them why it bothered them so much. Why did they care? They both looked at each other for a moment and then said, almost in unison, "Jack, to be honest, he's an embarrassment. It's hard to be proud of a son who is wasting away his life."

That phrase strikes a chord with many of us. "Turn out right." It's what we do this thing called parenting for, isn't it? So that our sacrifice, patience, and forbearance will be paid off by our kids moving out, getting married, starting a family (definitely in that order), and becoming adult members of society. Nagging in the back of our minds when our kids start adolescence and growing stronger as they grow older is the worry— for some of us it is a full-blown fear—that our kids won't turn out right. They won't achieve what we have planned for them. They won't make us proud. Instead, they will become an embarrassment, a millstone hanging around our necks. Often we feel guilty for even entertaining such thoughts. We wonder why we don't have more faith in our own children. We wonder if our expectations are too high, and we wonder if we are the only parents who feel this way about their kids.

The answer to that last question, of course, is that you are not the only parent to ever worry about your child's future. You are not the only parents who wonder if their daughter or son will ever make them proud. You are not disloyal or a bad parent for wondering if your child will ever learn to become a responsible adult. Every parent experiences these concerns at least a little. Even the most confident parent of a two-year-old listens to him struggle to talk and wonders if he will always lisp. Even the most understanding mother wonders whether her teenager will ever learn the meaning of the word "responsibility."

But for some of us this worry goes far deeper than an occasional twinge or a brief concern. For some it is a constant, deep-seated fear. We look at our growing or grown children and wonder if they will ever "turn out right." That phrase in all of its ambiguity is the only one that captures our fear. We aren't necessarily worried about drugs or sex, although sometimes that is a part of it. This fear is far less distinct than that. It is a vague feeling of unease that creeps over us when we think about our children. It is the slow flush that starts at the back of the neck and creeps up, when we realize that we don't really believe the boastful things we are saying about them. When we try to pin it down exactly, we can't. It is bigger than any one instance or action. It is a feeling of dread and failure.

What Do We Mean by "Turning Out Right"?

The first thing that we need to do, then, is to figure out what is behind this vague feeling. What is it really that we are afraid of? What we do mean when we say that we are afraid that our kids won't "turn out right"?

We asked parents across the country what they meant when they used that phrase. We asked them to try to nail down the fears behind the fear, so to speak. From their answers we

65

learned how this fear is played out in families like yours and mine.

To some families not "turning out right" means their children will not be successful in their careers. It means not having a certain standard of living—not owning a certain kind of house or a certain kind of car. Others were concerned about the prestige of their children's occupations.

Tied in very closely and mentioned often was the fear that our kids will not get the education that we desire for them, whether that is a college education, a master's degree, or something more. As a matter of fact, we surveyed parents and found that almost 90 percent worried about how well their children were doing in school. We become concerned for their futures when they drop out of college, do poorly in high school, or seem to put everything else in front of their studies. Often we have expectations that weigh heavily on us.

Denise is a popular high-school senior. As her senior year winds down, her parents are concerned that she hasn't applied for college yet. Finally after talking about it together, her mother and stepfather confront her.

"Denise, we were wondering when you were going to sit down and apply for school?"

"That's right, Honey. As a matter of fact, we're kind of worried that you won't get in if you don't apply right now. So I brought the forms. We can do them together right here."

"Mom, I'm heading out the door right now. I've got to meet Adam by 7:30. Can't this wait?"

"No, now I think that you're being irresponsible," her stepdad replied with an edge to his voice. "What are you afraid of? You're not leaving this house until these forms are filled out and signed. Now sit down!"

Denise looked from her edgy stepdad to her mom. They were waiting for an explanation, for a reply. She didn't know whether they could handle the truth, that she wasn't planning on going to college. At least not yet. She was going to go with Adam to Florida for the summer and then see what she wanted to do with her life. She decided that now was as good a time as any and blurted out her plans. Her mother looked as though she had just been slapped. Her stepfather got very red, and he spoke between clenched teeth. "I don't know what has gotten into you, young lady, but you are crazy if you think that we are going to stand by and watch you wreck your life. You are going to college, and you will do well."

Hours later, after the echoes of the yelling and tears had faded from the house, Denise's mom and stepdad lay in bed. Staring at the ceiling, both of them nurtured an unspoken worry. Finally, Fran broke the ice. "What are we going to do? She isn't going to amount to anything. I can't believe this is happening."

Her husband just shook his head, held her close, and said, "We're not going to let her do this, Honey. Don't worry." But even as he spoke those reassuring words, he felt a sudden stab of fear. After all, what could they do, really? Denise was already eighteen, an adult. She could do what she wanted, and they couldn't stop her.

Education comprises a large part of our dreams for our children. And, as we discussed in the last chapter, our dreams are pretty powerful things.

So not turning out right was about careers and education. But it was about more than that too. It can start when we witness our teenager starting projects and never finishing them. Or getting and quitting job after job. One parent expressed his worry with humor. "I'm a little concerned about my daughter's tendency to quit jobs. She is on her fifth one in about eighteen months, and frankly I'm worried that she is going to run out of fast-food restaurants and have to start over again."

At age sixteen I quit my after-school job at Kentucky Fried Chicken. My mother and father, upon hearing the sad (to them) news, recited to me a litany of everything I had quit since I was five. They then asked me, with a straight face, "Is this going to become a habit?" What they were worried about was that I wasn't going to turn out right. If I quit Kentucky Fried Chicken, wouldn't I also quit college? For many parents, the stirrings of fear are fed by such events.

Many parents worry about their child if he or she becomes resentful of authority or rebellious in actions and dress. We wonder if anybody will ever employ a kid with blue hair shaved on one side. Our friends tell us that it is just a phase and that they'll grow out of it. But we wonder. What if they actually like blue hair? What if they keep it blue forever? Blue hair definitely fits in the category of not turning out right for most of us.

"Turning out right" also includes our expectations for our child's family life. We are worried about whom they date or don't date. We worry if they date too much and if they date the wrong (to us) kind of person, and we also fear for them if they don't date at all. One father confessed that he thought his son might be gay because he showed a complete lack of interest in the opposite sex even though he was at the supposedly lusty age of sixteen. For most of us, having a gay or lesbian child doesn't fit the mold of turning out right. It didn't for this father, and one day he flat out asked his son, "Are you gay?"

To his relief, his son said, "No, I'm not gay. I just can't get a date, so why try?"

Our definition of "turning out right" usually has a great deal to do with the values our children choose to live by as adults and their choices about religion. I know that the biggest part of my parents' fear of my failing to turn out right was they were worried that I would turn from Christianity and never come back. We'll talk about that fear separately later on in the book. But it also plays a big role in this fear. Turning out right certainly is more than the right job or the right wife. For most of us parents the right values and beliefs are just as important, probably more so.

"Turning out right" includes turning out right socially. We don't want our kids to be nerds or geeks. We want them to be popular and well liked by their peers. We want them to be able to handle social situations. We don't want them to embarrass us in public. We want to be able to point across a crowded room to our daughter and smile with pride as we brag about her to our friends. We worry about our kids turning out right if they seem to be loners or unable to develop close friendships. We fear that they will go through life alone and unloved. Not our idea of a happy life.

At the bottom line, this idea of "turning out right" is often a combination of all of these things. But it can be boiled down into four general areas:

1. A satisfactory professional life, with the right education and career.
2. A good (read "normal") family life.
3. A stable spiritual life that echoes our own beliefs and values.
4. A vital social life, with friendships and a level of ease in social situations.

Perhaps the best way to illustrate this fear is to talk about my friend Rick and his youngest daughter. Rick is an elder at his church and a respected Christian writer. Others look to him for spiritual guidance. They trust his judgment, and they respect his knowledge of the Bible. Or at least they used to. Now, you see, they aren't so sure. Rick is struggling with his youngest daughter. Well, struggling is putting it mildly. He and his wife are on a collision course with her. She used to be like every other girl at their church, but in the past year she has changed. She cut her hair in a punk fashion, all shaved on one side and streaked with purple. She pierced her nose and covered her arms with tattoos. She began spending time with kids in their twenties, none of them high-school graduates, all of them a trying to be more outrageous than the other.

If that had been the end of it, it would have been okay, because Rick is a caring father and he lets Tracy have a long rope. But he could tell that her values were changing. She defied him and his wife openly about going to church and about their belief in God. She mocked them to their faces. She listened to music that turned their stomachs and then laughed at them for being offended. In short, they felt they were losing her. The first time I talked with Rick about his daughter he said something that really made me think. "You know what the biggest deal of this whole thing is?" he asked. "It's not the looks I get from coworkers or the subtle slams on my parenting. It isn't even watching Tracy wreck her life. It's knowing that everything I hoped for my daughter for the last seventeen years isn't going to happen, and I can't do anything about it. My daughter is a walking definition of 'not turning out right.' "

Rick's fears for his daughter couldn't be calmed by vague clichés or automatic referral to Scripture. He was scared, scared to death that his daughter wouldn't turn out right.

Why Is This Fear So Powerful?

The power that this fear has over us is largely a product of our expectations. Most of us have rather lofty goals for our children because in a very real way our children are how we judge our success or failure as people. Whether this is healthy or not isn't really the point. The fact is that many of us live out our dreams through our kids. We see their success or failure as our success or failure. As we grow older, many of us live out our lives through them, personalizing their triumphs and disasters as if they were our own.

So, if our children fail to reach the goals we have set for them, we feel like failures. We take responsibility for their mistakes. It becomes very difficult for us to draw boundaries between their actions and our parenting. Our self-esteem becomes dependent upon their accomplishments. This is not a particularly good place to find our self-esteem, but in our culture it is very difficult to avoid. One of our biggest fears, directly leading to this fear that our children will not turn out right, is the fear that they will reflect badly on us. If they do not achieve, it will be our fault. Others will look at them and blame us. After all, we all want to be able to brag about our children's accomplishments, big or small.

There is another aspect to this fear that makes it a powerful influence on our lives as well. We don't often talk about it because it seems crass and unkind. But for some parents there is a very real fear that their children will be dependent on them forever. Some of us wonder whether our children will ever be able to get along without our assistance.

Steve is a fifty-five-year-old executive with a nice house and a nice income. Divorced for many years, he has stayed friends with his ex-wife and has been an active parent. He has even gone to bat for his stepchildren, the product of his ex-wife's first, disastrous remarriage. But Steve has a problem. His oldest son, twenty-five, hasn't turned out as he planned. Instead, he has fathered a child out of marriage, now has responsibility for that child, and doesn't have the foggiest idea of how to take care of the child. Steve worries that his grandson isn't getting the care that he needs, so he sends occasional checks to his son, who has trouble holding down a job.

One day his son and grandson stood at his door. "Can we stay for a while? We don't have any other place to go?"

Steve thought he had no choice. He couldn't put his grandson out on the street. So he put them up for the night. "Just for a couple days," his son had said. But the days turned into weeks and the weeks turned into months. And fifty-five-year-old Steve was a parent all over again. His question: "When will my son learn to take care of his family? Will I have to provide for him forever?"

You may know someone like Steve, and his situation sends chills down your back because as you look at your child, you see some patterns developing that scare you. You wonder if he or she will be dependent on you forever. Added to that fear is the worry about who will take of you when you can no longer care for yourself. One aging parent put it bluntly: "How can he take of me, when he doesn't take care of himself or his own family?"

We wonder whether the time will ever come that we truly are on our own. We think about our dreams for our middle or late middle years. The empty house, the extra disposable income. We think about the trips we had talked of, the addition we had planned for the house. All of these plans are on indefinite hold, because our child or children haven't turned out right, and we are still responsible for them.

How Does This Fear Affect Us?

What this fear does to us is less important than what it causes us to do to our children. Our fear that our kids won't turn out right can cause us to do three damaging things to our children.

First, *it causes us to become overly sensitive to our child's failures.* Instead of allowing for failure as a natural part of growing and learning, we see failure as a beginning of a trend. Instead of understanding that failure is usually a precursor to success, we think that our kids are going to keep on failing. We tend to generalize their failures. One failure to follow through on a project and we find ourselves yelling at our kids that they never finish anything. One call from a teacher about goofing around in class and we tell them that they are "always in trouble." A single "C" on a report card becomes laziness. We push our kids to excel, to do better and achieve more, and when they fall short of our lofty goals, we think that they are headed down the road that will lead us to disappointment and embarrassment as parents. We think that a tough seventh-grade year means they aren't going to make it through high school.

I was speaking with a Texas teenager about her parents not long ago. She was an average kid in just about every sense of the word. She was a "B" student; she was fairly, but not overwhelmingly, popular and she played volleyball, but not expertly. Her mother, a medical doctor and exceptionally smart, kept nagging Tonya about everything. She didn't date enough to suit her mom. She didn't do well enough in school. She didn't excel enough in sports. And when she failed her physics midterm, her mother went through the roof. She couldn't believe that a daughter of hers could, in her words, "be so irresponsible and lazy." How else could she explain such a dismal failure? Her mother's words stung Tonya deeply. She spent a great part of her life trying to please her mom. But the words her mom ended the conversation with hurt Tonya even more. She said, "You are such a disappointment to me. You are never going to amount to anything." I looked in Tonya's eyes as she started to cry and saw what a parent's preoccupation with success was doing to a wonderful girl.

After talking with Tonya for some time and meeting and speaking with her mother, the underlying cause of this pushing to excel and achieve became apparent. Tonya's mother was very much in competition as a parent. She felt that in order to vindicate herself, her child had to achieve beyond what other people's children did. She was so worried that Tonya wasn't going to turn out right that she nearly destroyed her own daughter.

As we become overly sensitive to our children's failures, we tend to lose sight of the forest for the trees. We tend to miss the fact that failure is a terrific way to learn, and that a failure doesn't necessarily lead to a ruined life. As a matter of fact, for some teens and young adults, paying the price of failure is the only way to learn.

Many parents, concerned about their children's failures, spend a great deal of time peering over their kids' shoulders, making sure that everything is done right. Of course this kills initiative and creativity, but it does cut down on failure. The problem is that children never learn to pay the price for their errors when they are constantly prodded by a parent.

My mother and father tried often to teach me the value of responsibility and initiative. But I never wanted to do any more than I had to as a teenager. And my parents disagreed often about rescuing me from my mistakes, about letting me pay the consequences for my lack of judgment. Often my mother would wonder aloud if "I was ever going to turn out right." My father assured her that some people have to learn the hard way and evidently I was "some people."

One fall I was assigned the job of raking up the leaves in the backyard. We had several large trees, and the carpet of leaves was about six inches deep and covered our backyard. I hated raking the leaves and tried to do everything to get out of it. My dad was firm. "Jack, I don't care when you do it, but you will do it. And if I were you, I would do it before it snows."

Every day my mom would ask me if I was going to rake the lawn. Not my dad. He wasn't worried about failure or about my lack of responsibility. He had given his directive, and it was up to me to follow through.

Of course I delayed and delayed. One bright November morning I woke up to twelve inches of snow covering the ground. I walked downstairs and told my dad. "I was going to rake the leaves today, but it doesn't look like I will be able to. Look at all that snow."

My dad just smiled and said, "I don't care how much snow there is. It's your job."

I argued and threw a fit but to no avail. I wasn't escaping responsibility. Finally, after waiting two days for the snow to melt (it didn't), I shoveled *and* raked our backyard. It was at least twice as difficult a job with the snow on the ground. But I did it, and I learned a valuable lesson about procrastination.

If my father had been afraid that I wasn't going to turn out right and that my unwillingness to take responsibility for the leaves was just one more sign of my sure failure, he would have been looking over my shoulder, forcing me to rake the leaves in October. But he didn't, and that rather dumb move on my part helped me grow up.

Too many of us parents aren't willing to let our children fail and deal with the consequences. We think that every failure is ours and that it is a sign of worse things to come. So we push our children, driving them to succeed and excoriating them when they fail to live up to our expectations.

The second way we damage our children when we let this fear control us is a natural result of our inability to deal with their failure. *We damage their budding self-esteem.*

I related Tonya's story earlier. Her mother's relentless drive for perfection harmed her daughter's self-image. Tonya's mom set impossibly high goals, and Tonya's failure to reach them made Tonya learn only one thing: that she just wasn't good enough. And that lesson was one that would stay with her for a very long time. In fact, by destroying her daughter's self-image, her mother did a great deal to make her fears a reality, because it is hard to "turn out right" without a decent view of oneself.

Tonya saw that her mother's love was based on performance. She felt loved by her mom when she measured up to her expectations. For Tonya, her mother's love wasn't based on who she was, but what she did. This is not, I'm sure, the way Tonya's mom really felt. But we need to learn one very important thing about teenagers: they only know what they are shown. For them, to be loved isn't the same as to feel loved. And when we are only loving when they reach our performance standards, we are showing them that they are not to be valued for who they are intrinsically, but for what they accomplish. And that will kill self-esteem.

It is ironic that our fear that our kids will not grow into healthy, normal adulthood may end the one thing that helps them reach that goal—a healthy self-image.

By destroying their self-esteem we also inhibit our kids from trying new things. After all, if failure results in loss of felt love, and trying new things inevitably involves failure, then the safe thing to do is to avoid trying new things. Just as our kids are trying to figure out who they are, what they are good at, and what they like, our fear is keeping them from exploring the world. It is inhibiting them from finding out what their unique talents and abilities are. It is making them afraid to try, to learn, to grow. It is damaging their fragile, budding self-esteem.

The final way in which we can damage our children through this fear that they will not turn out right is when *we write the script for their lives.* We make our plans for our children and then expect them to live out those plans.

It is as if we are the directors of their lives and they are merely actors hired to carry out our vision. The movie isn't really ours. They are the writers, directors, and stars of their own lives, and they need to write their own special script. Instead, because we can be very narrow about what constitutes "turning out right," we try to keep them from failure by planning out their entire lives for them. And when they deviate from the script, often we become angry at them, as our fear rises up inside.

I was speaking to a group of students in West Virginia and gave a rather serious plea for them to give their lives in service to God. After the meeting I spent a great deal of time talking with these high-school kids from all over America. I remember especially an eighteen-year-old guy named Mark. Mark was what is know in the teen vernacular as a "stud." He was athletic, funny, and good looking. I had gotten to know Mark during the week and liked him immensely. After this final meeting he came with a serious look on his face and asked me if we could go somewhere quiet to talk. We did, and he began to tell me that he thought God wanted him to go to Bible school and become a youth pastor. He was almost absolutely sure of it, in fact. I smiled and told him that was great, that he would make a terrific youth leader. He looked at me, shook his head, and said, "But Jack, you don't understand. My parents have my whole life planned out. My mom has wanted me to be a veterinarian since I started taking care of stray dogs at the age of six. I'm already accepted to a great school. As a matter of fact, I'm leaving for freshman orientation in two and a half weeks."

I asked Mark if he had told his parents about God's call on his life. He shook his head again, "I can't, Jack. They are Christians and everything, but they would be so disappointed."

I left Mark that night and I haven't seen him since. I think about him once in a while though, and wonder if his parents realized what they were doing when they wrote the script for his life. Did they realize they were trampling on God's territory? I doubt it.

You and I are writing the scripts for our children every day. No matter what their ages, our fear that they aren't going to turn out right is causing us to plan out their lives for them. We don't trust them to make the right decisions so we hope to take all of the guesswork out of it for them. But in order to keep them true to the script, we end up manipulating, threatening, and forcing—and driving wedges into our relationships.

This can be a difficult fear for us to admit because it is so broad and so vague. Yet we believe that many of us are hurting our families with this fear. The fact is, we cannot make our children turn out right. That is their job. Our responsibility is to equip them with the tools to make good decisions and to help them establish worthwhile priorities. They have to do their growing up themselves. We can't do it for them.

Chapter Checklist

Complete the following checklist and talk about it with your family. Use this scale to answer each statement. Circle the number which best represents your answer.

1 = Strongly Agree, 2 = Agree, 3 = Undecided,
4 = Disagree, 5 = Strongly Disagree

1 2 3 4 5   1. I worry about my child's work/nonwork habits.

1 2 3 4 5   2. I worry about how well my child is doing in school.

1 2 3 4 5   3. I worry about my child's resistance to authority.

1 2 3 4 5   4. I worry about my child's social life (or lack of it).

1 2 3 4 5   5. I worry about my child's beliefs and values.

1 2 3 4 5   6. I worry about my child turning out right.

1 2 3 4 5   7. I wonder if my child will be successful in life.

1 2 3 4 5   8. I want my child to be successful in areas in which I did not excel.

1 2 3 4 5   9. I feel responsible for my child's success.

1 2 3 4 5   10. I feel like I have failed as a parent when my child fails.

Scoring: If you scored 20 or less, you are very concerned and may be fearful about your child turning out right. A score between 20 and 30 indicates that you are somewhat fearful (may have some real uncertainties) about your child's future. If you scored over 30, your concerns about your child's future success are quite normal.

CHAPTER FIVE

What Will the Neighbors Think?

The Fear That We Are Failing as a Family

It can be an overwhelming experience to walk into a bookstore and look at the parenting section. There are hundreds and hundreds of books, manuals, and magazines. They might offer a foolproof guide to child rearing or twelve steps to a happier teenager. These books and magazines hold out the ideal of the perfect, functional, happy family, a family that does everything right. Johnny and Jan do their homework. Mom and Dad are terrific and never frustrated. Even the dog seems well adjusted. When we compare what we read about with what we know to be true in our own lives, we see that there is a tremendous gap between what we are told we are supposed to be as a family and what we know we are.

We tell ourselves no one is perfect and then we gamely try to meet the latest expert's opinion of what a parent ought or ought not to do. Every book we fail to live up to, every magazine article showing us ten proven steps, and every radio program filled with good advice serve only to build up a deep sense of failure within us. A sense of failure *and* fear.

In a study we conducted with families we found that one out of five fathers is concerned with failing as a family. One out of five parents fears that they fight too much as family. One out of four adult males worry that their marriage troubles will hurt their children, and almost nine out of ten moms and dads are worried about how well they are doing as parents. We have seen the standard that is set for us as parents and families, and when we look at our own lives, we know that we are falling short. We know that we yell at our kids too much. We know our children are not respectful enough. We know that we don't pray together enough as a family or have family devotions. We know that we lose our tempers and become angry over small things. We know that sometimes our children are not wonderful. (In fact, sometimes they are downright surly and unpleasant.) We know our lives aren't neat and ordered. And when we see how far short of the expert's standard that we are falling, we become afraid, desperately afraid.

What is this fear that we are failing as a family? It is quite simply the fear that our inexpert parenting methods, our foibles and failures will ruin our children and their futures. Every time we turn on a television talk show, another strange guest with a very alternative lifestyle is blaming his parents for his affairs, her murders, or worse. After a while we begin to believe that it really *is* the parents' fault. We worry that one day it will be our children on "Oprah," and we will be on the hot seat. We feel like we are not measuring up to what a family should be and that there are dire consequences for not meeting the standard. Often this fear is fed by the industry that has grown up around child rearing, and it is further fueled by the well-meaning advice that Christian friends pass along.

I was speaking with a mother in California who was really struggling with her three children, all of them elementary-school age. A single parent with a limited budget, she never seemed to have enough to go around, and her kids were always asking for more. From time to time she would lose her temper and yell at her children. Afterward she would feel awful, like a failure as a mom. She asked one of the "good" moms at church how she could handle her anger more appropriately. The "good" mother told her, very seriously, "Well,

Carol, sometimes I'm angry with my children too. And you know what works best for me when I'm in a difficult mood? I pack up the kids into the minivan and drive to the ocean. Then we pray together as a family and ask God to bring us closer. Each one of the children pray and then I close. It always seems to do the trick. Now why don't you try it?''

Carol, who had been feeling moderately bad about her parenting, now felt infinitely worse. She knew that her kids would laugh her out of their beat-up old Honda if she even suggested the idea. She was trying to find a way to keep from throwing things at her children, and this woman wanted her to hold devotions!

When I met Carol, she was convinced that not only was she a bad parent but a terrible Christian as well. Now I'm not condemning the practice of praying with your children. As a matter of fact, I recommend it highly. But it isn't where Carol is at, and all that advice did was reinforce her feelings of failure. It confirmed her suspicion that she and her children were failing as a family.

Many times in our public speaking, my dad and I hear from people who are concerned that they are failing as a family because they aren't living a textbook family life. Often they say, "We don't communicate well." We ask them how they should communicate and they don't really know. They just have a feeling that the way they are doing it is wrong and that there must be a secret out there somewhere that everyone else knows about except them. Sometimes families feel they are failing because they fight too much. One father, after spending a weekend on a parent-teen encounter with us, felt they were failing because they didn't fight enough!

We worry that we aren't disciplining enough or that we do it too much. We worry that we are too angry, too young, too old, too insecure. The bottom line is that we feel that there is a "right" way to parent, a "right" model of a family, and whatever we are, we aren't "right."

Why Do We Feel This Way?

Beyond the specifics of our failures, there are two basic reasons why we feel that we are failing as a family. The first reason is the *expectations* our culture places upon parents.

At the end of the twentieth century we have done a very good job of taking personal responsibility away from our children. Turn on the television any weekday morning and listen to the litany of problems that are blamed on parents. It can seem that almost any mistake a person makes is traced back to some flaw in the way he or she was raised. This puts enormous pressure on us to do the right thing. Of course the problem is that often we don't know what the right thing is. We don't know how to respond when our child shoots his dart gun at us for the thirtieth time after we have told him to stop. We don't necessarily know what is the right choice for the thousands of decisions we make as parents every week.

And it doesn't help to read the parenting books and magazines either. It seems that one on discipline says "Spare the rod; spoil the child." Another points out the great evil of corporal punishment. Both writers are Christians. Both of them claim to know what godly parenting is. How do we judge what is right?

My dad was speaking with a father one afternoon who had come to him for some help with his parenting. He was having a very difficult time with his teenage son. His son was into the party scene big time, and his father had caught him coming home drunk. So Carl grounded his son for one month. It was a serious punishment for what Carl believed was a serious offense. Until his son's youth pastor called Carl. "Mr. Roberts, I'm wondering if you're not being a little too hard on your son. He's just growing up. . . ."

Hanging up the phone, Carl was sure that once again he had blown it. After all, didn't they pay the youth pastor to understand teenagers because regular people never could? The youth pastor must be right. So Carl prepared to lift his son's grounding. But he made the mistake of telling his father what he was going to do. And Grandpa was sure that Carl had let his son off too easy. He thought that Carl should ground him for three months.

Now Carl was thoroughly convinced that he didn't know how to parent. He was sure that they were failing as a family and that it was his fault. So on that afternoon he poured out his heart to my dad. And Dad asked him a simple question: "What do you think is a good punishment?" Well, that threw Carl for a loop. After all, wasn't Pastor Schreur, the family counselor and author, the expert? So Carl acted like it was a test and tried to get Dad to reveal what the right answer was. But Dad just said over and over again, "What do you think?" Finally Carl couldn't stand it any longer.

"Pastor, you're not really being much help at all here. I need to know what to do!"

My dad smiled and said, "Carl, you are the parent. You know your son better than his grandpa does, better than his youth pastor does, better than I do. You also know what is acceptable and unacceptable behavior. You have to make the rules and dole out the punishment. You can make a good choice here. I believe in you." Carl was blown away. The idea that he as parent might actually know what to do was a new idea to him.

Such is the result of living in a culture where we put great weight on what so-called "experts" tell us we ought to do. We listen to them tell us what we are supposed to be like as a family, and we feel awful when we fall short of the goal.

I remember hearing a Christian leader talk about his family problems, trying to make the point that even he had struggles as a husband and father. So he told a story about how he had blown it. It seems that his teenage son had come home thirty minutes after curfew one Saturday evening. Dad waited up for him and grounded him for a week. His son tried vainly to explain why he was late, but this Christian leader would have none of it. He went to bed with his son still angry. The next morning he got up and apologized to his son for not listening to him. The leader then looked his audience of several thousand in the eye and said, "You see, even I blow it sometimes."

I sat in the pew and tried to figure out exactly where he had blown it, because being unfair and angry and not listening seem to me to be part of everyday family life. Now it was admirable of this man to apologize to his son, but I think most of the people in the audience felt the same way I did. *Wait a minute. He thinks* that *is messing up. I'm in real trouble here. I'm trying to keep from strangling my son when he wanders in three hours late with no explanation, and this man's problem is that he let his son go to bed angry at him? Oh my!*

Most of us are trying to get the big things in our family right, and when a guy comes on television and tells us that is all he struggles with as a father, we slide a little lower in our chairs and our self-esteem takes another dive because we know that we struggle with so much more.

Unwittingly, we follow a simple syllogism to determine our own failures. Well-known Doctor X says that good Christian families don't fight. We fight in our family; therefore, we are not a good Christian family. Or Pastor Z says that good, loving families have morning devotions together. We don't have morning devotions together; therefore, we are not a good, loving family.

You get the idea of how it works, don't you? It goes like that for almost everything we've ever heard. We fail to live up to the expectations that our culture places upon parents and walk away feeling like failures. After we've read every book and tried every twelve-step program to wholeness as a family, we still can't achieve that mythical "good Christian family," and we feel worse and worse. Every new book adds to the weight on our shoulders and soon we are convinced that we cannot do anything right. That is the first main reason we feel like we are failing as a family: the *expectations* of others and ourselves.

The second reason we fear that we are failing as a family is the *observations* we make of other families. This works in two ways. First, we look around us and see many failing families. We hear about them on TV and radio. We read about them in the newspapers. The divorce of a family member or close friend can cause us to think, "First them, now us."

After a particularly wounding argument, we feel that we must be next on the list of families about to disintegrate. We must be headed for divorce court as well. There is so much talk about family dysfunction, and we look at the people who say they are from dysfunctional families, and their backgrounds are just like ours. When their families remind us of ours, we begin to feel a sense of hopelessness. We can start to believe that no matter what we try, it won't be good enough. After all, if so-and-so didn't make it, why should we? All of the statistics and stories cement in our minds the impossibilities of raising a healthy, together family. When we couple that sense of futility with a strong sense of what we are doing wrong, we are soon headed down the road to the fear that we are failing as a family.

The second way in which our observations cause us to feel like failures is that sometimes when we look around our church and at our friends, we don't see anyone who is like us. They seem to be perfect and without blemish. When we compare what we are with we what we see in them, we're sure we're blowing it.

Growing up as a pastor's kid, I remember looking at other PKs and thinking that some of them were perfect. They just never did anything wrong. I was in trouble all the time. They were in church all the time. At one point in my life I felt like I was a failure as a kid. Why? Because I didn't measure up to what I observed in others. Not until much later, when I found out what really went on in some of those "perfect" PKs' lives, did I realize how mistaken I was.

We can be the same way with our families. "Oh, I'll never measure up to being as good a father as the pastor." Or, "She's such a good mother. She's home all the time; she bakes; she makes her kids' clothes. Here we are on our fourth pizza of the week because I don't have the time or inclination to cook. I guess I'll never make it."

Our observations are not very accurate. We are only seeing

what others choose to let us see. We aren't really looking at the whole picture. But it doesn't matter — it still leads us down the road of fear. We fear that we have somehow missed out on the secret of parenting children that everyone else knows.

How Does This Fear Affect Us?

This fear does awful things to our self-esteem and our confidence as parents. We go through our days with a heavy weight on our back, knowing that one day our children are going to have to pay for all of our failures as parents. We feel that the day of reckoning is just around the corner, waiting to leap upon us. This fear profoundly affects us in at least three ways:

1. We feel guilty.
2. We feel inadequate.
3. We feel frustrated.

We feel guilty.

In our effort to try to become the perfect parents, we always fail. And in trying and failing over and over again, we build a tremendous sense of guilt. Many parents who are struggling with fear are constantly burdened by guilt. They are constantly worrying that it is all going to catch up with them. To relieve their guilt they often take responsibility for every bad thing their husband, wife, or child does. The logic goes like this: *It's not really Brad's fault that he failed algebra this year. If I hadn't been working, I would have been home more to help him with his homework, and he would have done just fine. The real failure was mine, not his. He doesn't deserve to be punished. I'm the one who caused his problem.* To some of us that seems a little extreme, but in our years of working with families Dad and I have seen it over and over again. This feeling of guilt, induced by fear of failure, makes parents take responsibility for their children's failure and lack of achievement.

This sense of guilt causes us to look for atonement anywhere we can find it. One father who worked long hours and traveled often felt that he was failing his kids because of his job. So whenever he was with them, he showered them with things. At the movies they were the kids with the huge buckets of popcorn and all the candy they could stuff in their mouths. They went to every amusement park and always bought cotton candy. This father was trying to atone for his guilty feelings.

Some parents atone by trying to become Supermom or Superdad. Nancy was an angry woman from a terrible family background. As the parent of three young boys and a girl, she found her anger coming out unexpectedly and inappropriately. Guilty and worried that they were failing as a family because of her background and her inability to deal with it, she tried to make up for her "mistakes" by being Supermom. She volunteered for every possible school outing, was den mother for Girl Scouts and Cub Scouts, helped teach children's church, and did her best to make sure that her children never had to deal with the real world.

The sad thing is that Nancy's smothering mothering drove her children and even her husband away from her. None of her children went on to live for God. Two of them are divorced, and one of them hasn't spoken to any other family member in four years. Once again, as we have seen so often before, the irrational acts that our fears push us into often make our worst fears come true.

Guilt can also destroy our marriages. When one marriage partner is giving everything that he or she has to "make the family work," there is often a lack of real intimacy. Activity has been substituted in its place. Instead of a quiet evening with just the husband and wife, a fear-driven father will insist on making it a family day at the beach while the neglected wife fumes silently. This drive to overachieve brought on by feeling guilty can hurt a marriage relationship. One husband put it rather succinctly when he said, "I don't know if she does stuff for me because she loves me or because she thinks that's what she has to do to be a good wife. It seems that our marriage has become all form, with a hole in the middle where true friendship used to be."

We feel inadequate.

Wes has packed the kids off to Grandma and Grandpa's again. He and his wife are headed downtown for a seminar on how to be great parents. It is the fourth seminar this year that Wes and Diane have attended. Once again they listened to expert speakers, took copious notes, and promised to do better. But when they picked up the kids and reached home, the same old feelings hit them. Wes felt completely inadequate as a father and husband. He just wasn't up to the demands of the job. And the more he read about it, the more seminars he attended, the worse he felt. It was as if he was going backward in his quest for proficiency at parenting.

Wes's feelings of inadequacy are at least in part caused by his fear that he is failing as a father. He has read all the newest books on fathering, and, well, it just seems to him that he will never measure up. He looks at his children and realizes that he will fail them, and he wonders if he will ever be the kind of man that they can be proud of. When he fights for sleep in the dark, the thoughts keep pounding him. *You'll never make it! You aren't strong enough! You don't know enough! You are going to fail!* Wes feels terribly inadequate. His fear is eating away at his self-esteem.

It wasn't always this way for Wes. Once upon a time, he had been fairly confident of his abilities as a dad and husband. But as his children started to grow, he began to look around at other dads, and they seemed to be so much more involved with their children than he was. They seemed to have discovered the secret to fathering that had eluded him. The more he thought about it, the more a fear grew in his heart that he was failing his kids, that they were going to have to pay for his failures later in their lives. And the more his fear grew, the more it ate away at his increasingly fragile self-esteem. This in turn fed his fear and further damaged his self-esteem. Caught in a vicious, unending circle, Wes looked all over for help. He went to every seminar, read every book, and even attended a men's conference that involved living in a teepee, grunting, and getting in touch with his "wild man." But nothing seemed to help. He still felt like a failure.

This fear of failing as a family will kill our self-esteem. And the more we try to learn, the more we will find out that we are doing wrong. That doesn't mean that seminars and books are bad. As seminar leaders and authors, we feel that there is much to be gained from both. But they aren't going to help you with the root cause of your distress. The root cause isn't that you don't know enough to be a dad and you never will. The job defies our efforts to learn it. It *is* hard. The root problem is your fear. And your self-esteem will continue to erode until that fear is handled properly.

We feel frustrated.

The net result of this fear of failure is frustration. After we have been to every seminar, read every book, and listened to every radio program, we realize that we are still making mistakes as parents. And every time we try a foolproof parenting tip, we find out that our kids are the exception to the rule.

I know that I frequently frustrated my parents when I was growing up. I was not a perfect child and had to be disciplined often. Mom and Dad grew tired of spanking me because it seemed to have little effect, so they decided to send me to my bedroom every time I disobeyed. That, by the way, was deemed the perfect punishment by the Christian parenting expert of their day (who shall remain nameless). The only problem was that I liked going to my room. Although I was a very social child, I was also an avid reader, and going to my room for hours afforded me the opportunity to read and read. My parents finally figured out that sending me to my room wasn't going to work when they had to threaten me to get me to come out. My parents had found out that their child was the exception to the rule.

Frustrated parents are not usually good parents. And as our frustration at our failures grows, so do our failures and mistakes. Once again our fear has us in a "no-win" cycle that is very difficult to break out of. As our self-esteem gets worse and worse, we tend to generalize our perceived failures as a parent or spouse into other areas of our lives, and pretty soon it seems that we aren't capable of doing anything right. This adds to our growing frustration, which often erupts at our families, causing us to feel even more like failures.

Those who were raised in difficult family situations feel history repeating itself and feel powerless to stop it. Pam grew up in a home without a mother, and her father was an angry, despairing man. Nothing that his children did was good enough, and the smallest failure was enough to set him off on a tirade of verbal abuse. Pam grew up despising and fearing her father, vowing that when she had kids she would never lose her temper at them. Her anger at her father never went away. She even refused to go to his funeral because she felt that it would be hypocritical.

After she married and became a parent herself, Pam noticed a disturbing trend. She tended to react to stress just like her father. She didn't yell and scream as he had, but she could feel her anger boiling up inside. It scared her to death. Her first thought was that she was going to be just like her father. She knew how much she had despised her own dad and she began to fear that she would fail in her quest to be different. She worried that her kids would feel the same toward her as she had toward her own father.

Pam compensated for her fear by trying to be the best and most understanding mom that ever walked the planet. She was always in control on the outside, never letting the anger that surged within show to anyone. Finally, she could no longer contain it and it burst forth upon her unsuspecting family like an overburdened Mississippi levee. She was ashamed and horrified and vowed to try harder, but soon enough she blew up again. It happened over and over, and each time she lost her temper, her fear of failing as a parent grew. She became

90

more frustrated with herself, which contributed to the struggle she was having with anger. Until one night she sobbed into her pillow, "I'm just like him. I'll never do better. My kids will be just like him. Can't I escape my past?"

Our fear that we are failing as a family is a powerful force in our lives. It causes us to feel extreme guilt, even though we are just being human. This guilt causes us to take responsibility for our children or our spouse instead of doling it out where it belongs. We rob them of what they need to become mature and responsible human beings. Then our fears for our family become reality.

Our fear harms our self-esteem. We feel inadequate and unable to deal with the pressures of being a wife or mother, husband or father. We look for the perfect method to parent, and when that fails, we blame ourselves. We always think that *we* are the problem, that others don't fear and worry as we do. We are sure that others are not making the mistakes we are.

Finally, the fear of failing as a family results in frustration. As every solution and quick fix turn out to be dead ends, we become frustrated and feel trapped in a vicious cycle of failure. Often this causes our fears to come true.

It doesn't have to be this way. It is possible to escape from the relentless treadmill of failure that our fears have put us on. In Part Two of this book we'll show you how to break the cycle of pain.

Chapter Checklist

Complete the following checklist and talk about it with your family. Use this scale to answer each statement. Circle the number which best represents your answer.

1 = Strongly Agree, 2 = Agree, 3 = Undecided,
4 = Disagree, 5 = Strongly Disagree

1 2 3 4 5   1. I worry that we are failing as a family.

1 2 3 4 5   2. I worry that we fight too much in our family.

1 2 3 4 5   3. I'm afraid that our marital problems will negatively impact our children.

1 2 3 4 5   4. I feel that I'm failing as a parent.

1 2 3 4 5   5. I feel very inadequate as a parent.

1 2 3 4 5   6. I get very frustrated trying to live up to the expectations of others.

1 2 3 4 5   7. I think that other families are doing much better than we are.

1 2 3 4 5   8. I hesitate to share with other parents and friends how my children are doing.

1 2 3 4 5   9. I sometimes think that God never intended for me to be a parent.

1 2 3 4 5   10. Our family is not doing very well.

Scoring: If you scored 20 or less, you are overly concerned about how well you are doing as a parent. A score between 20 and 30 indicates you have some concerns or maybe are not sure about how well you are doing as a family. If you scored above 30, you probably have average concerns about your parenting abilities.

CHAPTER SIX

The End of Our World

*The Fear That
We Will Lose Our Children
through Illness, Death, or Serious Accident*

Margaret hurried home from work through the cold and drifting snow. Her car was warming up slowly in the frosty night air, but the chill in her heart wouldn't go away. She was so afraid that something had happened to her daughter Mandy. The baby-sitter hadn't phoned and she had no real reason to be afraid, but she had a feeling deep down inside that her daughter was going to be hurt. Finally, arriving at her baby-sitter's, there was Mandy, safe and sleeping soundly. Margaret picked her up and held her close, the fear within subsiding at last.

That night, long after her husband had drifted off to sleep, Margaret lay awake. *Why am I so worried about Mandy?* she thought. *Why do I always have this terrible feeling that she is going to die?* As she fell asleep, she had nightmares about her daughter and a burning house. She woke over and over again wet with sweat. But the dream persistently stayed with her until morning.

Across the country Tom had lain awake that night as well. Sleep was something that was becoming more and more of a stranger to him. As a single father trying to raise a teenage son and daughter, he had a lot of legitimate things to worry about, but lately it seemed to Tom that he was worrying more and more about his children's safety. His son was out with the church youth group on an overnight camping trip, and he couldn't believe how worried he was. He called and checked the messages on his machine four times in an hour while he was working late. Expecting to hear the worst, he was almost surprised that there wasn't a message of disaster on the answering machine. Now, late at night, he decided that he wasn't going to let his son go on any more overnights. There was just too much potential for accidents and mishaps. He listed the possibilities to himself: There could be a car accident. They could drown in the river. They could get Lyme disease from a tick. He went on and on, and as the list grew longer, his determination grew stronger. He was going to protect his kids. He wasn't going to let them die or be seriously hurt. He wouldn't allow them to get into situations that were potentially dangerous.

Many of us have looked at parents like Tom and Margaret and wondered what was wrong with them. We may have thought of them as overprotective, dismissing their problem with a simple, "They're just really concerned about their children." But Tom and Margaret do have a problem. Both of them are paralyzed by the fear that their children are going to be taken from them through a serious accident, a rare disease, or some other catastrophe. Their fear is more than just a normal concern for their children's well-being. They are almost certain that whenever their children are out of their sight they are in danger.

As a youth pastor in Michigan, I experienced this kind of irrational fear through a family in our church. They were neat, caring people who truly loved the Lord. But Lois was incredibly fearful that something was going to happen to her children. When her oldest child reached junior-high age, Lois refused to let her attend most youth group functions for the simple reason that many of them started at the church and finished elsewhere. She didn't want her kids riding in the church bus. Her fear didn't diminish as her children grew. It grew right along with them. It got to the point that she wouldn't let her twelve-year-old daughter cross the street without her. Needless to say, at that point her husband and daughter began to realize that something more was at work in her life than simple parental concern.

Most of us don't go to the extremes that you have just read about. But many of us are haunted by the fear that our children will be taken from us. We have watched the news and seen enough TV movies to know that it is possible. We may know someone who has lost a child, and we wonder why it hasn't happened to us. In our survey of family fears we found that almost half of all parents described themselves as worried about their children dying or being involved in a serious accident. And the fear doesn't stop with us, the parents. Many children and even teenagers list losing a parent to death as the top fear they have. Why is this fear such a powerful force in our lives? Why does it exert such control over us?

There are, of course, as many reasons for this fear as there are people who are living with it. It is a highly individual worry that we often try to hide from others. But the reasons boil down to three basic categories. We are afraid that are children will be taken from us because of our nature, our nurture, and our negativism.

Nature

Our nature causes us to fear a child's death because we know that life is fragile. It is in our nature to fear that what we love most will be taken from us. For some of us, that fear works out into a healthy, precautionary concern. For others, it becomes irrational and even paranoid.

One parent we met believed that her child was going to die in a car accident. When we asked her why, she said, quite simply, "Because I don't deserve to have her. She is too perfect." I thought about that for a while and spoke with her a little later. It was in this woman's nature to believe that anything good that happened to her wouldn't last long. Her nature, her self-esteem, told her that she didn't deserve good things. And the best thing in her life was her child. So naturally she believed that her child was going to be taken away as well.

Maybe that extreme a reaction doesn't strike a chord with most of us, but even my own wife, who is pretty normal, worries about losing one of our kids. When I ask her why, she says something to this effect: "Because our life is too good, Jack. We've got a great family, and we love what we do. Something has to go wrong."

It is natural for us to assume that if everything is going right in our lives, it is time for some tragedy to strike to bring us back down to reality. What could be more full of tragedy than the death of a child? This cause for fear cannot be dismissed because it sounds slightly ridiculous when we talk about it in the bright of day. When we are in our beds at night and sleep is far away, many more of us have thoughts similar to this than we would like to admit. We lay quietly fearful that the next morning will bring not a new day, but a tragedy. When the morning breaks bright and clear and everything is all right, the previous night's fearful musings are conveniently forgotten . . . until the next time.

Nurture

Perhaps the primary cause of this fear is our nurture, the way we were raised and the way we were taught to look at life. If you were raised by fearful parents and were taught to be afraid constantly, because you could never tell when the next tragedy would strike, it is very likely that you have carried this with you into adulthood.

My mother was, and still to a lesser extent is, afraid that either my brother or I was going to die. She was at times almost paralyzed by that fear. It played a large role in her decision-making, in what she allowed us to do, and what she said no to. This fear stems in large part from my grandmother. My mom was raised to fear. She was taught to fear. When she was five, her father went in for routine surgery and died on the operating table. She never said good-bye to him. We related earlier in this book how to this day my mom cannot take leave of us or our families without a good-bye hug and a word of love. She is afraid that what happened to her father will happen to us. Her nurture, the way she was raised and the things she experienced as a child, affect her profoundly and cause her fear.

Others have been raised in overprotective environments and have taken that with them into their own parenting. If our parents were fearful and overprotective, then even if we vow to be different, it is very hard not to follow in their footsteps. Their way is the only way that we know. We haven't experienced models of confident parenting so we struggle to parent confidently. It is natural to fall back into the fearful parenting styles that we have known since childhood.

Negativism

The final broad category of causes for our fear is negativism. Quite simply put, we look at the fragility of our children, especially our young children, and we don't believe God will protect them. We don't believe God is in control. We have seen too much "evidence" to the contrary to rest peacefully knowing God is the creator and sustainer of life. Our negativism fuels our fear that our children will be taken from us. We become suspicious of God and His motives, although we certainly would never admit it. I remember one young father who was struggling mightily with his fears for his children. He said: "I know in my heart that God loves me and my kids and wants the best for us. But I can't help worrying that He might use us in some cosmic power play, just like Job." Maybe not the words of faith that we mouth on Sunday mornings, but certainly true for him.

Our negativism says the world is a cold, hard place, and our children are small and unprotected. We look around us and see possible accidents around every corner. Every trip to the grocery store involves flirting with death because of our negativism. We simply think the worst is going to happen and we don't trust God to keep us from it.

What happens when we are in slavery to this fear? How does it work its way into the seam of our everyday life? Well, obviously we tend to be overprotective. We see a threat to our children's well-being where there isn't one. We take enormous responsibility on ourselves to ensure their safety. We tend to be omnipresent as well as overprotective. We hover over our children as much as possible because only we truly know how fragile they are and how dangerous the world is. This overprotection can come out in simple ways, like never allowing our kids to do what other children their age are doing.

Growing up, I had a friend named Peter who never climbed trees with us or built forts up in the trees. His mother forbid him to climb trees. She was afraid that Peter would tumble out and that would be the end of him. So he would just amble on home whenever we got it into our minds to climb trees and build a fort. We all felt sorry for him. Even at eight years old, we knew he was missing out and that it wasn't his fault.

In this day of headlined sexual abuse and abductions in every neighborhood, parents have wisely become more safety conscious. But we have to be careful that this safety awareness and the legitimate caution that it engenders doesn't become an irrational fear. My daughter Erin wanted to bring one of her friends home from school with her, a friend that she had spent many hours with at the friend's house. So we called her parents and asked if Mickey could ride home on the bus with Erin. Mickey's mom said that she didn't think that was such a good idea. So we asked the following week. Same answer. Not easily dissuaded, Erin asked again the next week, and for the third week in a row was told no. I asked Mickey's mom why she wouldn't allow her daughter to ride home with Erin. She said, "I'm just not very comfortable with Mickey riding the bus. I pick her up from school every day. I guess I'm just an old worrywart, but I always worry that the bus will get in an accident. So I don't allow Mickey to ride it." I asked her if

Mickey had been to any other children's homes this school year. "No," she replied. "We do have a lot of her friends over here with us though."

As I hung up the phone, I realized that her fear made her deny her daughter the opportunities that other children her age had. As a matter of fact, a case could be made that Mickey was missing an important ingredient in her socialization. She never had to deal with a family and other people outside her own circle and her own home. I felt sorry for her then and wondered if her mother's fear was showing up in other places as well.

Our overprotection is not the only result of our fear. We also show a marked lack of trust in God. We've touched on this subject before and will again later in the book. But for our purposes, here let's just say that our fear, as it becomes irrational and extreme, denies God His rightful place as the creator and sustainer of the universe. In a very real way we think we know better than God. We want our way and not His way, and we become irrationally fearful that His way is going to result in the death of one of our children.

We have every right as parents to worry about our children. I do. Sometimes I worry about them a lot. We have every right and even the responsibility to take precautions and to do every reasonable thing to help ensure their safety. But that is the key word: *reasonable.* We can't guarantee their safety. And we will do tremendous damage if we insist on trying. Death can and will strike. Often it seems completely random and wanton. The child who dies of leukemia, the baby born with spina bifida, the teenager in the car accident. We've seen it in our own families, in our friends', and in the newspapers. And everything in us cries out that's not going to happen to our children, not if we can help it. We resolve to do everything we can to ensure their well-being, and slowly, silently this irrational fear gains a foothold in our lives.

When does legitimate concern become a malignant fear? There are no formulas or scientific symptoms. Ask yourself what is controlling you. Is it your fear? If you look at the actions you have taken over the last six months and they seem to be arbitrary and filled with anxiety, look deep within for the fear that is beginning to control you. This fear can wreck a child, a marriage, a family. It cannot be allowed to run unchecked.

The Results

The end results of letting fear control us are many and far-reaching. Our children grow up without skills—some that only come with a degree of risk—because they were never allowed to try anything new. They can't throw a football, because we were afraid football was too rough. They can't drive on snow as adults because as teenagers they were never given the keys when the white stuff was covering the ground.

My dad took me aside a few weeks ago and asked me if he could teach my children to shoot a BB gun. He had bought a little one on sale and had it up at their cottage. I told him I would have to talk to Leslie, since guns are a rather touchy issue. I was pleasantly surprised when my wife said, "If your dad wants to take the time to teach the children about guns, I'm all for it." I was surprised because I really thought that the danger element would worry her. But she said something very interesting. "I would rather have them learn what guns can do and have a healthy respect for them as well as the proper way to handle them. I think that is probably the best way to avoid an accident." She's right, of course. And by getting past her fear, she is taking steps to ensure that her fears will not come to pass.

Think with me for a moment about what could happen if Leslie and I gave in to our fears and told my dad not to teach my children about guns. They would never learn the gun safety that my dad taught my brother and me. They would never learn to respect the firepower of a gun. They wouldn't know how to check if one was loaded or even what a safety on a gun looked like. If they were shown a gun at a friend's house, how much more at risk would they be? Once again, our fears can keep us from doing the truly safe thing.

Children who come from fear-controlled homes not only grow up lacking vital skills, they also grow up fearful themselves. They perpetuate the fear from generation to generation. Their parents were brought up by fearful parents; they have been brought up in a fear-driven home, they repeat what they have learned, and the cycle goes on and on without a break.

The lack of competency and the fearful attitude that children learn becomes a negative force on their self-esteem. The fears of their parents contribute to a poor self-image and a lack of confidence. After all, if your father is constantly telling you that you can't do this because you might get hurt, or you can't go over to so-and-so's for the night because it is raining out, or you can't play in Little League because the ball is hard and you really aren't much of a hand with a glove anyway, how is that going to affect you?

Positive self-image is especially important during the middle years of childhood between ages six and twelve. It is during this time that our children need desperately to be good at something. Erik Erikson, the developmental psychologist, says it is during this time that a child develops either a sense of industry (capability) or inferiority. Our fears can keep our children from gaining the competence necessary to develop this sense of industry. The result is a sense of inferiority, of not being able to do anything well. This lack of self-esteem will come back to haunt our children during their teen years, and then some of our other fears will be played out before our eyes.

Children who come from fear-driven families will also miss out on educational opportunities. I take a group of high-school students into the inner cities of America each summer for a missions trip. We want to help students see the world that exists outside their doors and to help those who often cannot help themselves. This past year we went to Los Angeles and stayed downtown in the skid-row area. As we were preparing to go, the mother of one of my students phoned. Her daughter wanted to go with us very badly, but she was legitimately concerned. After all, Los Angeles certainly isn't the safest place in America, and if you are from a farm in western Michigan, it feels like a foreign country.

As I talked with this very nice woman, I became aware that there was more going on than just a legitimate fear. She kept pressing me for more and more safety precautions. Finally she said with an air of finality and resolve to her voice, "I can't let Barbara attend unless you can guarantee her safety." I said quite firmly that since I couldn't guarantee her safety crossing the street in front of her house, there was no way that I could guarantee her safety in L.A. I assured her again that we were doing everything we could to make the trip as safe as possible, but that it was a learning situation and that learning situations have an element of risk.

To that mother's credit she allowed her daughter to grow and learn. Many of us do not. We let our fear stop our children from learning. They miss out and sometimes come to resent us because of it.

This brings us to another result of this fear. Sometimes our children will spend their adolescence and early adult years in a "rebellious" seeking out of what has been denied them. They are resentful of the control we have exerted over them and of the fact that we have denied them things unfairly, so they engage in what we call rebellion. But this may be more than rebellion. It's acting out against our fears. It is proving us wrong, even if it kills them.

These teenagers become very confused. If everything, even relatively normal things, are wrong and potentially dangerous, then how do they judge what is really wrong and really dangerous? When driving to school is forbidden because of a parent's fear and so is drinking alcohol, we have equated in our teenager's mind driving to school and drinking alcohol.

Needless to say, this kind of confusion doesn't make the teenage years any easier for teens or their parents. Their confusion is a direct result of our confusion. We are the ones who first mixed up what was truly dangerous and what wasn't. It is only natural that our children will mix it up as well. Instead of seeing everything as dangerous and potentially harmful, they may see everything as benign and harmless. We have sown the seed for this type of behavior when we spend all of our time trying to protect them from things that they don't need to be protected from. They lose their perspective just as we have lost ours.

Children who grow up in homes controlled by parents' fear of losing them often lack a sense of adventure. That natural adventurous and mischievous spirit was killed by the relentless fear of their parents. Every time a child shows his natural adventure he gets scolded or warned, and Dad or Mom just about goes off the deep end. Pretty soon the child will learn to stifle his inquisitiveness about the world because it is getting him into too much trouble. As adults, these people are, quite frankly, boring. They lack the gleam in their eyes and exhibit an unhealthy reluctance to try new things. They pass along those inhibitions to their own children and perpetuate the cycle of fear.

These children also never learn to balance risk and reward. Almost everything that we do as human beings is a carefully or not-so-carefully thought-out equation of risk versus reward. *If I take that promotion, I'll have more responsibility, more control, and greater freedom. But I'll also have a greater chance of failure and no one else to blame it on. Is the risk worth the reward?* If we grow up in homes driven by this fear, we learn by example that all risk is to be avoided, that the reward is never worth it. This kills creativity and the drive for excellence. Because with every new opportunity and every fork in the road, there is risk *and* there is reward.

Ultimately we don't want to be controlled by this fear because it turns us into what we don't want to be. We become suspicious, overprotective, untrusting, and even unfaithful to God. We turn our children into either rebellious teens acting out their resentment of our control or lackluster adults who are missing that vital spark and gleam that is so infectious and enjoyable. We miss out on the best times with our kids when we let this fear take control of us. When we are living in fear of their lives, we don't let ourselves have fun or even really let go with our kids. There is a certain reserve that can crop up in our relationships. It is very difficult to love wholeheartedly when there is an irrational voice inside telling you that the person will be taken from you.

My dad has never let his fears control him, sometimes much to my mom's chagrin. But because of that he enjoyed my brother and me immensely and we enjoyed growing up with him. We still spend a great deal of time together (like writing this book), building on bonds that were forged when we experienced great things together when I was a child. Now he is enjoying his grandkids in much the same way that he enjoyed us, and they love him back with abandon.

Dad built a zip line in the backyard two years ago for his grandkids. That's right, a zip line. In the backyard of their cottage my parents constructed a huge jungle gym. And off the end of the jungle gym my dad attached a large steel cable to a tree, about twelve feet off the ground. He attached the other end to another tree about thirty feet away and only three feet off the ground. The cable has a pulley and a handle. The kids climb the jungle gym, wrap their hands firmly around the handle, and swing out all the way down the cable. *ZZZZzzzzip* is the sound it makes as they fly into the sandbox that serves as their landing area. That's why it's called a zip line. Of course, he takes precautions. He guides the kids down, especially the little ones, but he never lets his fear interfere with a great time. Our family is the better for it, and our kids will have stories to tell their children.

Don't let your fear spoil your parenting. It is a sobering thought to think of our children dying or being seriously hurt, a thought that often haunts me in the darkness and the quiet of night. But we can get beyond it. We can live though our fears. We can let God take control. Keep reading as we close this part of the book with a look at one more fear and then move into how to overcome our family fears.

Chapter Checklist

Complete the following checklist and talk about it with your family. Use this scale to answer each statement. Circle the number which best represents your answer.

1 = Strongly Agree, 2 = Agree, 3 = Undecided,
4 = Disagree, 5 = Strongly Disagree

1 2 3 4 5   1. I hesitate to allow my children to take normal risks like other children.

1 2 3 4 5   2. I often worry that one of my children will suffer a serious accident.

1 2 3 4 5   3. I was overprotected as a child and not allowed to do what other children were doing.

1 2 3 4 5   4. My child resents me because he/she is not allowed to participate in certain activities with others his/her age.

1 2 3 4 5   5. My child seems to be very fearful of any activity which involves risk.

1 2 3 4 5   6. I tend to be an overprotective parent.

1 2 3 4 5   7. You "can't be too careful" with your children.

1 2 3 4 5   8. Our family often argues about participation in risky activities.

1 2 3 4 5   9. If my child is late coming home, I worry about his/her safety.

1 2 3 4 5   10. My child tells me that I worry too much about him/her.

Scoring: If you scored 20 or less, you are probably overly concerned (fearful) about your child's safety. A score between 20 and 30 indicates that you are somewhat fearful or anxious about your child's safety. If you scored over 30, your fears are probably quite normal.

CHAPTER SEVEN
Between Heaven and Hell
The Fear That Our Children Will Not Live Out Our Values and Beliefs

Pastor Scott cried silently as he hung up the phone. His wife looked at him with great fear in her eyes. "Scott, were they calling about Ron? Have they found him? Is he all right? Tell me what's going on!" Scott wondered how he was going to tell his wife that their oldest son was dead, a victim of AIDS, brought on by a promiscuous homosexual life-style. His mind raced back over the years, images of Ron as a young child playing with his race cars on the living room floor of their first, tiny parsonage. How wonderful their life had seemed then. He had been such a trusting and beautiful boy. Scott's eyes stung with tears as he remembered how the congregation at that small country church had taken them under their wing and helped them with the medical expenses surrounding Ron's complicated, expensive birth.

Scott remembered the move from that small church to the mega church that he pastored for many years. Had that been where things went wrong? It was hard to say because he had been so busy. He had been the pastor of a church that was growing by leaps and bounds, from 1,000 members to over 3,000 in just five years. Scott had been gone a lot and had missed much of Ron's grade-school years. All the conferences he had spoken at, all the words of praise that he had heard were empty now, as he looked back and realized that his only son was gone and that he had never really known him at all.

Marjory looked at her husband and knew that her son was gone. It was the look in his eyes, the pain on his face. They couldn't really say that his death was unexpected. They had known for more than a year that their son had the HIV virus. They had sat in shock and disbelief as he told them over the phone. He had been slightly mocking even then. They had invited him home to die, but he had just laughed. They begged him to ask God for forgiveness, to get his life right with the Lord before he left this world, but again their pleas had been met with nothing but laughter and sarcasm.

Marjory listened to Scott relay the news of their son's death and as they embraced and held each other, her mind went back to Ron's high-school years. That had been the hardest time in her life. She remembered the first call from the principal at the Christian school run by the church Scott pastored. "Marjory, this is Hank at the school. We've got a problem with Ron. He just won't do his homework for Bible class." That was the first of many calls, each of them more serious as Ron began a descent into unbelief and a lifestyle that would eventually result in his death.

Her flitting mind came to a halt at the memory of that awful day when as a college freshman he had told them that he was gay. They had wanted to pray with him and to hold him, but he told them that he didn't believe in God anymore, that their faith was just another fairy tale. They had asked him to seek counseling to overcome his struggle with homosexuality. He had replied cuttingly, "What struggle? I'm proud to be gay. This is the way I am and I can't change it. I don't even want to!"

Then from the car had stepped his lover, a man in his forties. They were moving to the West Coast, where Ron could finish his college and they would be free from harassment. With that, Ron turned and walked out of their lives. They heard bits and pieces from Ron's old friends, and he called his sisters once in a while, but for six long years he never called them, never wrote to them, and they didn't know whether he was dead or alive. Then came the brief, mocking call, relating to them the news that he had AIDS. And now this call from one of his friends. "Your son is dead. The funeral was yesterday. He didn't want you to be there. That's why we waited to call."

Scott and Marjory's story is being repeated across the country every day. The details are all different, and AIDS doesn't play a part in every one of them. But every day people you and I know are facing the fact that their children have grown up and are not going to live out the faith that they were raised with. Every day mothers and fathers are coming to grips with the fact that their children do not share their beliefs and values. And as we hear their stories and watch those dramas play out in their lives, we are desperately afraid we are next. After all, if someone like Scott can't raise a child who follows Jesus and lives out his father's values, who can?

For many of us this fear is the most powerful of all the family fears. It certainly is the one that holds me most in its grip. I worry about many things, but my deepest fear is that my three children will grow up and not become followers of Jesus. I fear they will reject the faith of our family and our values. I know my parents wrestled with the same fears, and not without good reason.

At seventeen years of age, I had done a lot of thinking and reading, and I had decided that Christianity didn't make sense to me anymore. I didn't want to tell my dad because he would have been profoundly disappointed in me, and I wasn't sure how he would react. But I was getting really sick of church and all of the trappings of Christianity, and so one day I told my Dad that I wasn't sure about all of this "God stuff." He just looked at me and asked me why, and we talked for a while. Emboldened by his mild reaction, I told him that because I didn't believe in God anymore it didn't make much sense for me to have to pray before I ate. He just smiled and said okay. I went a step further and told him that I didn't think that I should have to go to church anymore either, since I didn't believe what was taught there. Once he again he looked at me without expression and said okay. Feeling pretty good about my tough stand against my father's beliefs, I turned to walk out of the room when he called my name. "Jack, by the way, where are you planning on staying?"

"Uh, what do you mean, Dad?"

"I was just wondering where you were going to live?"

"I'm going to live right here," I replied with an uncertain tone.

Dad was not uncertain. "I don't think so. If you want to live in my house, you play by my rules. And our rules are that we pray in this house and we go to church. If you are a part of this house, you will do the same thing."

"He then looked back at his book, and the conversation was over. I stood there for a while trying to think of something to say. But I had exactly eighty-nine cents in my pocket and twenty dollars in the bank. I knew I wasn't going to get far, so I stayed and played by his rules.

When Dad and I speak about family fears, we tell that story and it usually provokes a sympathetic laugh from the audience. But now I know the anguish and fear those kind of remarks caused my parents. They were very worried that their oldest son was going to abandon the faith. My father and mother used every opportunity to impress on me the importance of being a Christian and living out Christianity's values. But I didn't want to listen to them, and their fear grew as I got older and began to make decisions about who I was going to be, what I was going to do with my life, and what I was going to believe.

What is this fear, the fear that our children will not live out our faith and values? Why is it so powerful in our lives? And how does it affect us? In the next few pages we'll answer those questions, showing how this fear can grip our lives, change our families, and ruin our relationships. We'll relate stories of others who have struggled with this fear. Some of them have won; some have been overcome by it. Through their lives you will be able to see how this fear affects you and how it is working in your family.

What Are We Afraid Of?

This fear is about what our children believe and how they behave. We know their beliefs will affect their behavior, and we want them to have the kind of beliefs that encourage right behavior. Because this fear is not just about what they think but also how they act on this thinking, it is often entangled with our other fears. For instance, as we see our children grow up and make sexual choices we don't approve of, we are often worried that they are going to make a life-dominating mistake because they do not share our family's values about sexuality. If we knew they shared our values and beliefs about sexuality, we wouldn't be worried nearly as much about the life-dominating mistake.

This fear is in many ways the root fear that we have for our children. We worry that the things that are important to us will not be important to them. We fear things we have tried to teach them over their lifetimes will be left behind as they move from childhood into adulthood. We fear their lifestyles will reflect badly on us, that others will see our children are not living out our values and that we will be considered bad or ineffective parents. We worry they will become enamored of some cult or weird system of beliefs. We are concerned about the influences unbelieving teachers and professors have on their lives.

The long and short of it is that we want our children to value what we value, to hold dear the same things we hold dear, to love God as we love God, to follow Him as we try to follow Him. We want them to follow us into heaven and to walk in our footsteps of belief here on earth as much as possible. We fear that somewhere along the way as we are walking along merrily, assuming our children are following along nicely behind us, we will turn around and see they are gone. We worry that somewhere back down the road they will have stepped off the path and be gone forever.

Cheryl was an active member of her youth group, a part of the discipleship team and student leadership team. Lindsay was proud of Cheryl, proud of the way she was turning out, proud of the fact that her daughter was following Jesus. Cheryl was excited about her impending graduation and enrollment at a Christian college. Everything was working out just as Mom had hoped, until one day Cheryl came to her Mom's room late at night and wanted to talk. "Mom, Dad has invited me to come and live with him in California. I love you and don't want to go, but if I establish California residence I can go to UCLA and film school. Mom, I really want to try to become a film director. So I think that I'm going to move in with Dad."

The conversation went on for hours, and then continued over the next few days. But Cheryl was eighteen and legally the choice was hers to make. As she watched Cheryl board the airplane for the long ride to L.A., Lindsay wondered what would happen to Cheryl. Would she find a church and keep following Jesus, or would she fall away as her father had done? And how would she handle the pressure of being a Christian at a place like UCLA's film school? She wasn't sure, but it sounded like a terribly immoral place to her.

Lindsay fought off an urge to run after her daughter and beg her not to leave. She stared at the plane as it slowly moved away from the gate, trying hard to catch a glimpse of her daughter in the window. Walking to her car, Lindsay was struck by the fear that Cheryl would leave more than just home.

Lindsay is struggling with fear because of what she knows and what she can't know. She knows that her ex-husband is not a Christian. She knows that he will not encourage Cheryl to attend church and find a group of Christian friends. She knows that the UCLA film school isn't going to be a Christian environment. She doesn't know how serious her daughter is about her faith. She doesn't know how her daughter will handle the pressures of college. She doesn't know how her daughter will deal with the immorality around her. The combination of knowledge and ignorance creates a tremendous fear.

Why Is This Fear So Powerful?

Lindsay and Cheryl help us illustrate why this fear holds so much power over us. It is one thing for Cheryl to tell her mom that she doesn't want to attend a Christian college. Lindsay could live with that. But what she is wondering is if by turning her back on a Christian school, she isn't really turning her back on her faith. And Lindsay is too serious about her Christianity to be able to live with that.

When we think our children are going to reject the values and faith that they have been brought up with, we get scared because we know just how important values and faith are. We know that what a person believes will determine how that person acts, and we know that turning away from God and rejecting Christ has eternal consequences. My dad put it to me this way: "Jack, when you were growing up and we lived in Chicago, your mom and I loved the Cubs. We hated the White Sox. We taught you to love the Cubs and to despise the White Sox. But if you had turned to me at sixteen and said, 'Dad, I like the White Sox, but the Cubs stink!' I could have lived with that. It wouldn't have been easy, and I would never have understood your reasoning, but I could have lived with it. But when you had turned to me and said, 'Dad, I know that you are a pastor and that Christianity is important to you, but I don't buy it,' well Jack, that was something we not only couldn't understand, it was something that troubled our sleep and caused us great fear. Because who you are is so much a part of what you believe. And because we knew that the choices you were struggling with had eternal consequences."

There are four reasons why this fear is so powerful in our lives. We have talked about some of them through the stories in this chapter. Stating them clearly, they are:

1. Values and beliefs have eternal consequences.
2. Values and beliefs are intergenerational.
3. Values are personal.
4. Values matter.

Values and beliefs have eternal consequences.

We have touched on this truth several times already, but let's note it clearly here. As followers of Jesus we know what we believe matters. We know decisions our children make during adolescence can lead them to heaven or hell, and that alone is enough to make us afraid. This is not, as my dad said, about which baseball team to cheer for. This is quite literally a matter of life and death. Our fear is that our kids will make the wrong choice and that we will spend eternity separated from them.

This is not an irrational fear. Many children do grow up and leave their parents' value system. Many children grow up, never believing what their parents assumed they believe. Many kids in churches today have no intention of following Jesus when they are "released" from their parents' rule. They have no desire to go to church, to study the Bible, to do the right thing. They are just marking time until they are out on their own and can live the way they want.

Our worry is that our child is one of "them." We don't want our kids to be the ones to toss off faith like an old overcoat as soon as they are free of our influences.

Values and beliefs are intergenerational.

When we were writing our book on grandparenting, one of the refrains we heard from nearly every grandparent we interviewed was that they wanted their grandchildren to grow up in the faith. One of the deepest fears many of these older saints had was that their grandchildren wouldn't follow Jesus because their parents weren't serious about Christianity.

This family fear is powerful because we know it doesn't just affect our children. The values our children choose will affect our grandchildren, and their children, and on down the line. A lot is at stake here. And when we stop to think about it, we become frightened. The intergenerational ripple gives us pause, and fear wells up in our souls for unborn grandchildren and their faith.

Often our values and beliefs are what we most want to leave behind when we are gone. On a national radio talk show that Dad and I were guests on the host surprised my dad by asking him what he wanted to be remembered by. He answered simply and clearly, "I want to be remembered as being faithful to God and my family." Those are my father's core values. Those are things he hopes will stay with us long after he has passed from this earth.

The talk show took a personal turn when the host asked if that was the way I would remember him. With tears in my eyes and a lump in my throat, I replied, "Yes, my father will forever be remembered as faithful to us and to his Lord."

After the show was over, I thought about that question and realized most of us would like to be remembered for our core values, the things we hold dearest and true. And that is one of the reasons why this fear threatens us so much. The idea that our children will reject our core beliefs shortens and diminishes our legacy, perhaps the only legacy worth leaving.

Values are personal.

The fear that our children will reject our values or beliefs is powerful because values are personal. If a child rejects my values, he is rejecting a very big part of me. Our children are not only trampling what we hold to be right and true but are disowning us as well.

Ted was a good Catholic. He took his church, his faith, and the values that he had learned at St. Mary's High very seriously. He never missed Mass and truly loved Jesus. When Ted overheard his daughter on the telephone talking about "going on the pill" to one of her friends, he was almost beside himself with anger. Fueling that anger was a profound fear that his daughter was going to reject the values and beliefs that had sustained his family for generations. He was, however, not a talkative man and didn't know how to handle the situation. When Ted came to us, he was almost choking with grief.

"I can't believe it, my own daughter. Living in sin. Does she think that I was such a jerk for all these years of believing? For trying to honor God?"

We talked for a while about how he could handle the situation, and I mentioned that it didn't necessarily mean that his daughter was having sex, but that he ought to talk to her right away.

He began to cry and waved his hands for me to be quiet. "What is killing me about this is not that she is having sex, or that she is thinking about having sex. It's that she knows how wrong I think this is, how wrong God says it is, and she doesn't care. She's not only turning away from Him, she is turning her back on me!"

Many of us share Ted's feelings.

Values matter.

We know ultimately that values and beliefs make a difference in the way we live our lives. They make a difference in the way we raise our children, the way we treat our husbands and wives. They change the way we do business, act toward authority, and handle our resources. In short, values matter. This culture doesn't want our children to get that message. America at the end of the twentieth century would have our children believe that it doesn't matter what they believe, just as long as it works for them. That is why our teenagers don't understand when we get so worked up about them attending church or youth group. They are being prodded by society into believing that values really don't matter.

We know better, and that is why we are afraid. We know our children's beliefs and values will shape their lives. We so desperately want them to grow into people who are a force for good in this world, a force for God, that we are afraid when they tell us, "What difference does it make if I believe in Jesus or not, Mom? I'll still be a good person." Or when we hear them say, "Dad, don't get so worked up. She had an abortion. It's all right now." We know it's not all right, because values matter.

How This Fear Affects Us

The fear that our children will not live out our family beliefs and values is a valid one. It is perfectly legitimate to fear for your children's souls in a cultural climate like ours. Every time I think about this subject and think about my three children, I worry. I fear they will not follow their father and grandfather in the faith, that they will not follow their mother and grandmother's values. I get a sinking feeling when I think about what the consequences of their decisions could be. Because of my fear, I may do many things that will drive my children away from my values and make my nightmares reality. As a parent I want to think for my children, to take all of the hard work of value formation away from them. I know what I want them to believe, and I know that if I let my kids think for themselves they might not end up believing what I do.

Let me illustrate this principle in a simple way. My son Jonathon is almost five years old. He loves to play soccer, basketball, and baseball, and he loves to watch those sports on TV. When it comes to baseball, I love playing catch with him and help him learn to hit the ball. But I hate soccer. Well, hate is too strong a word. I guess I have more of a cordial dislike for soccer. My real love is football. I'm glad that my son likes baseball, but I'm more than a little disappointed that the kid has shown no interest in football. He doesn't like it on TV. He doesn't want to play with one. He won't even touch it. Instead, he kicks the ball around, soccer style.

In my desire to see him like football as much as I do, I keep telling him how much better football is. I tell him soccer is for people who aren't coordinated enough for football. (I know it's not true, but hey, I'm on a mission, right?) When I ask him what he wants to do and he says, "Play soccer," I tell him I won't play with him. When I turn on the TV and he refuses to watch the Monday night game with me, I try to bribe him into it. You know what the end result of all of that manipulation is? Jonathon hates football more than ever and is now beginning to question baseball.

We treat our adolescent children the same way. We want

them to believe what we do so much that we bribe them, entice them, try to do all of their thinking for them. As a result, our kids move farther away from our beliefs at the end of the process than they were at the beginning.

When this fear grows to dominate our lives, we refuse to let our children think for themselves, and in so doing, don't allow them to make our values their own. The principle task of adolescence is identity formation. What that means is that during the teenage years our children decide what they are going to be and believe apart from us. What they need to do is to examine the values they have been taught since they were children and then decide to make those values their own. They need to adopt them and claim them as their own ideas and beliefs.

There is always the danger that during this time of separating what they really believe from what they have been taught to believe they will toss away the things we hold important. It must be this way. If there is no real risk of them rejecting those values, then they are not really owning them. Only when they honestly sort out what they hold to be true from we have told them is true do they achieve the identity they will need to make it as adults.

This process scares us to death. It is fraught with danger. The "what if's" will haunt our sleep. What if they don't believe in God? What if they don't believe in marriage? What if they don't believe in a good education? The "what if questions" really boil down to the one big one: *What if they don't believe what I want them to believe?* What will I do then?

In order to avoid having to answer that question, we try to tell our kids what they believe. We operate under the old "When I want your opinion, I'll give it to you" rule. We don't allow for any freedom of expression, because every time we hear something that we don't agree with, we think our children are abandoning our values.

Growing up in the home of a successful, well-known pastor and Christian educator had its ups and downs. The up was that my parents were terrific. The down was that they were still normal parents. But they had the added expectations for values that deeply spiritual people place on their children. I rebelled at the very conservative theology of my father (the same theology I now hold dear, by the way) and began to experiment with some decidedly non-Christian belief systems. As I related to you earlier, I eventually decided that I didn't believe in God.

My mother went fairly crazy during my time of wrestling with doubt and unbelief. She was quite reasonably afraid that I was going to become a skeptic and stay one for the rest of my days. She asked my father many times to try and force me into the "right" way of thinking. But he never did. He answered every question about God that I put to him with honesty and vulnerability. I asked the unanswerable like, "Why is there pain and suffering in a world created by an all-powerful and loving God?" He never hid the paradoxes or the difficulties.

One day while we were driving together and talking, I realized how generous he had been in letting me find my own Christianity apart from his. I thanked him for the space he'd given me to try to figure out what I believed. He just smiled and said that everyone needed to own their faith. And that if mine was just inherited from him, it wouldn't be worth very much at all.

I said, "Dad, you know I'm only eighteen years old. I know that Mom is pretty hyper about some the dumb things I've been saying."

He smiled and nodded at that one.

"But Dad, being eighteen, don't I have the right not to be right about everything? Don't I have the right to still be putting this stuff together?"

He looked at me and smiled his warm and gentle smile and said, "Jack, you not only have the right, you have the responsibility to put it together yourself. I'll help you as much as I can, but the bottom line is that it's your job. And your faith won't be complete unless it is really all yours!"

My dad was right. But in our fear that our children won't

follow us into the faith or won't share our treasured values, we don't give our kids their responsibility. We want to take it from them and do it for them, but it won't work. What will happen is our kids will grow up without anchors. They won't know why they believe, and they won't live what they say they believe because they don't really own it. In ten years of counseling teens I have met with many students who go to church every Sunday, never miss youth group, and never say or do anything unchristian in front of Mom and Dad. But they do not care about God or know Him in a personal way. They play the game because they have learned that it is much easier to say the right thing than to work out what they really believe.

That is one of the reasons that college students and young adults have such a shallow faith. They were never allowed to make their faith their own. This process involves doubt, questions, and hard truth. Instead, they went along to get along and never really believed anything for themselves. Is that what we want our kids to do?

Do we want them to be the kind of people who know what they believe and why? Do we want them to be able to defend their values and their faith? Or do we want children who say the right thing but are missing the real heart of the matter? Our fear that our children will not live out our values and beliefs can cause us to deny them the very thing they need to truly live out those values and that faith: the freedom to accept it or reject it. They need the freedom to explore it for themselves, to test its validity, and to see if it is real. I know it sounds scary, and it is, but it is the only way.

As a young youth pastor some years ago, I sat in my office and listened to a very angry couple vent their frustration with me, the church, our pastor, and our youth ministry. At one point in what turned out to be a very long evening, Melissa looked at me and said; "You told our daughter that she had to grow up her faith, that the faith she had as a sixth-grader wouldn't carry her through adulthood. When she came to you for guidance at a crossroads in her life, you actually sent her away from God!"

Those hadn't been my actual words, and the context was missing, but they were right. I had told their daughter that she needed to grow up her faith. Her parents had told her that literally everything she needed to know spiritually she had already learned by kindergarten. They told her if she had any doubts or if she questioned anything they told her about faith and values, she was sinning. They were so afraid that she wouldn't make the right choice, their choice, that they forbade her to disagree with them.

The epilogue to the story is sad. One daughter is suicidal, claiming she wants to be a missionary one minute and doubting the existence of God the next. Their oldest daughter no longer shares what she believes with her parents. She knows how bad they will be hurt if they found out that she had abandoned the faith she had been brought up to honor. It didn't have to be that way, but when our fears are controlling us, we are not rational. This fear, more than any other perhaps, drives rational thought out of our minds.

This fear can be especially devastating when our view of the right thing is very narrow. Every idea that differs from ours is attacked as heresy and sin. When our children ask innocent questions, questions that they need to have answered with thought and gravity, we tell them just to fall in line and follow us. When they bring up alternatives that are well within the Christian tradition but not exactly as we see them, we threaten them with everything but the kitchen sink. Perhaps that sounds extreme, but I have seen it happen, and in his twenty-five years of ministry my dad has seen it too often. Families are destroyed over a nonessential doctrine. Or over voting for the "wrong" candidate.

Our fears that our children will not live out our values and faith make us extremely controlling, and when our children rebel at our control, we claim that they are in sin and threaten them with God's judgment. Our kids repay us by "sitting down on the outside and standing up on the inside." When they leave our care, they leave our carefully constructed values behind as well, because those values are not theirs. They are still ours.

121

What we really accomplish by trying to force our children to believe every jot and tittle that we believe is to send them out into a very scary world without any armor of belief of their own. We are not preparing them to "give a ready answer," but to parrot our answers without conviction. And when those answers no longer work, they abandon their faith or their values. Often our fear has played a role in that decision.

Chapter Checklist

Complete the following checklist and talk about it with your family. Use this scale to answer each statement. Circle the number which best represents your answer.

1 = Strongly Agree, 2 = Agree, 3 = Undecided,
4 = Disagree, 5 = Strongly Disagree

1 2 3 4 5   1. I worry that my child will marry a person of another faith.

1 2 3 4 5   2. I worry about some of my child's statements about the Bible.

1 2 3 4 5   3. I worry about my child giving in to the "spirit of the age."

1 2 3 4 5   4. I worry that my child's lifestyle will not reflect my values.

1 2 3 4 5   5. I do not allow my child to express disagreement about or question my religious beliefs.

1 2 3 4 5   6. I often worry that my child will grow up and reject my religious beliefs and values.

1 2 3 4 5   7. I am deeply concerned about my child's lack of interest in spiritual things.

1 2 3 4 5   8. My child does not seem interested in church attendance.

1 2 3 4 5   9. I cannot talk with my child about spiritual things without an argument or disagreement.

1 2 3 4 5   10. My child is already making choices that do not reflect my religious values and convictions.

Scoring: If you scored less than 20, you have deep concerns about your child living out your values and faith. A score between 20 and 30 indicates some concern and uncertainty. If you scored above 30, you have fairly normal concerns about your child living out your faith and values.

When Our Worst Fears Come True

Inevitably some of our fears will prove valid. Our children may make life-dominating mistakes, and we will be left wondering how to salvage them from the wreckage they have made of their lives. One of our kids will leave the faith without a backward glance, and our last word of him or her will be from the police. You may come home one day to a note on a pillow, "I had to go, couldn't take it anymore. My lawyer will be calling." The tragedy of divorce will be played out in a place you never expected, your own life. The point is that eventually some of the things you most fear will happen. How will you handle it? How will you cope when your worst fears come true?

It happened in our family. Here is our story. I was the wild child. I was the one who everyone expected to make a life-dominating mistake. I was the one who played around the edges of danger. It was in my nature to be rebellious, to push whenever my parents said pull. I walked as close to the line as possible, and even stepped over it occasionally. My brother Jon was, in many ways, a perfect teenager. He didn't drink, didn't smoke, didn't even date much. He was a straight "A" student. I mean straight A's. The kid never got a B in his life. He was disciplined and faithful. He never questioned church or our family's belief system. He was what every mother wanted in a son.

He didn't yell and throw things. He was respectful. In short, Jon and I, while best friends, were complete opposites in high school. Twelve months separate me from my brother. And all of our lives we have been close. We are so different that he never had to handle much comparison with his older brother, and because I was older, I never had to deal with teachers who wished that I would pay as much attention to my studies as he did. We were close, until he went away for his first year at college. He went to Michigan Technological University, almost thirteen hours away from our home by car.

We only saw him occasionally that first year. But my parents were so proud of him. He had earned a full scholarship to MTU because of his diligence in high school, and he was going to earn a degree in electrical engineering. My father was proud, my mother almost bursting. When he returned home each break though, we could tell that something was changing. My brother was growing up. He wasn't the acquiescent child he had been when he left. He was beginning to question things that he had held sacred his whole life. His grades, while acceptable, were not sparkling. My family didn't worry about him though. He was still Jon, and everyone knew he would do all right.

On completing his first year of college and returning home, my brother was a different man. And shortly after he returned home, I found out at least part of the reason.

"Jack, I need to talk to you about something."

"What is it, Jon? What's bothering you?"

"Well, do you remember the advice you gave me about dating? About what I should and shouldn't do?"

"Yeah, I don't remember saying much, just to keep your pants zipped."

"I, uh, well, I didn't exactly follow your advice."

"You mean that you and what's her name, your girlfriend up there, you, uh, did it?"

"Yeah, we did."

I walked around our big stone porch and wondered what to say to my little brother. He had just jumped way past me in his knowledge of sex. Then it hit me. This wasn't all he wanted to tell me.

"Jon, is Lynn pregnant?"

"Uh, well, that's kind of what I was getting at, Jack."

"Do Mom and Dad know?"

"I told them last night. We don't know what we are going to do."

That was a bombshell, dropped without warning on our perfect family. Well, we knew that we weren't perfect, but we didn't believe that this would happen, at least not to Jon. My relatives had all assumed that something like this might happen, but they all believed that I would be the culprit. My parents hadn't had a great deal of time to worry about my brother. They were too busy worrying about me. When he brought home the news that his girlfriend was pregnant, their world stopped for a moment. One of their worst fears, that one of their children would make a life-dominating mistake, had happened. Of course, the fact that it was Jon and not Jack was a surprise. Most of their fears had been reserved for me. But the one thing my mother had worried about since my birth nineteen years earlier had happened. The question was how were we going to deal with it as a family.

The moment is still etched in my father's mind. Jon was subdued, quiet. "Dad, can you and Mom come downstairs? I, we, Lynette and I need to talk to you about something. Uh, I don't know how to say to this, but Lynette is pregnant."

Mom said, "You're kidding, right?"

"No, I'm sorry, but it's true. We found out for sure this afternoon."

Dad's head spun as he groped for the right word. The feelings of disappointment, anger, and betrayal crashed in on him. "Jon, we love you. I don't know what else to say."

"Jon, I want to know something. How could two people who are so smart be so dumb?"

I don't know, Mom. We always thought that we would stop,

that it wouldn't come to this. I'm so sorry." Then the room was quiet. Jon left to take Lynette home, and Dad and Mom were alone with their fear.

How is he going to finish college? Are they going to keep the baby? What about marriage? Jon was a full-scholarship engineering student. *Will this endanger his scholarships? And what about Lynette? How will she ever succeed as a metallurgist?*

Then they had some sobering thoughts about the effect on their own lives. "What will people think of us? Jerry, you're a pastor. This isn't supposed to happen to you. You are the family counselor."

"I don't know what people are going to say. I can't think about that now. We have to help Jon and Lynette. We have to love them through the next few months. And we have to make sure that Jon doesn't pile mistake upon mistake."

Research shows that during times of family crisis, some families — strong families — actually come together and grow closer. It is as if the fears that had been harbored by parents alone are now out in the open for everyone to see, and they are shared equally by everyone. That is what happened to our family. While others counseled Jon and Lynette to get an abortion, or shrilly ordered them to get married immediately, our family came together to try to find the best way through this difficult time. It wasn't easy. Everything in us urged us to push the panic button.

My parents struggled with feelings of anger and hurt. Their natural tendency was to blame Lynette for what happened. After all, how could their perfect son be to blame for a mistake as big as this one? They struggled with trying to control Jon and Lynn. After the shock had eased, it seemed right to make Jon's decisions for him, to straighten out the mess that he had made of his life.

Mom and Dad didn't know how to face their friends or family. There was a very real sense of shame that descended on our family for a while. There were whispers behind my Dad's back at church. There were angry words spoken between Jon and me. There was tension in our house. Overall there was an ache that didn't want to go away. It sort of wore on us as that summer wore on. But we didn't crumble as a family. We didn't give up, and through it my parents learned how to cope when their worst fears came true.

There are lessons to be learned from our story, lessons that can provide hope for you when your worst fears come true. In a very real sense when our fears are proven right and that which we dread has happened, we go through some clearly defined stages of loss. Not everyone experiences every stage, but for most of us this is the pattern of feelings we go through.

This Isn't Happening to Us!

Our first feelings are ones of shock and denial. *My son can't be a father out of wedlock. He's my son, and he wouldn't do that. My daughter can't be using drugs. She's too smart.* Our minds recoil at the thought that this is happening in our families. Even though we may have had a very real fear that something was going to happen, when it does, we can't believe it. We know that bad things only happen to other people. So our first and strongest reaction is to deny it.

This can cause us to be very self-protective. Struggling to come to grips with the reality of the situation, we tend to withdraw or to push others out of our lives. In our denial we want play ostrich, to stick our heads in the sand and hope that the trouble will all go away. In our denial we may throw our children out of the house, saying things that we would never say when we are rational and thinking clearly. But the feeling that "this can't happen to me" makes us want to remove the source of the problem, to avoid thinking about it, and our children's presence is a reminder of the reality of the problem.

Why Is This Happening to Us?

After denial runs its course—and for some of us that may take a long time—we come to the questioning phase of handling

129

our loss. In our family we simply wondered why something like this would happen to a good Christian family. My parents wondered why my brother, so perfect in high school, had made such an about-face in college. They wondered where they had gone wrong and if they should have let him attend a state university. Most of all, they looked at the sky and asked God the unanswerable question, "Why have You done this to us?" They were disappointed in God. They had kept their end of the bargain. They had done their best to raise their children with the values and morality of the Bible, but because of one failure the whole family was having to pay. It didn't seem fair.

Of course, in their wondering and their disappointment with God, there was another dynamic at work. Because my father was a well-known minister, he had to pretend that these doubts weren't there, that he was fine with the lot that God had given him. But inside he didn't feel like working, like teaching, like preaching. He felt like having a face to face with God.

As we struggle with reality when our worst fear has come true, we tend to look beyond the choices that we or our children have made and blame God directly. When our son is arrested by the police for dealing drugs, we may get angry at our child, but often we direct that anger right at God. When our daughter is pregnant, we tend to look past the obvious reason and look at God and ask why. We feel like Job, who couldn't figure out why God's hand of protection had been lifted. And like him, we demand an answer of God.

The truth, though, is that we are not Job. He was part of a cosmic power play, of God revealing Himself in all of His power and majesty. For most of us the answer to the question, "Why is this happening to me?" can be answered with a simple, "Because the choices you or your child have made bear consequences." In our family it was easier to blame God than to look my brother in the eye and say, "You made a big mistake." So we questioned God and His love for us. Job's problem may not have been our problem, but God's answer still applies: "Where were you when I laid the foundations of the earth?"

Must This Happen to Us?

As reality sinks in, we move to a position of bargaining. As we deal with our loss, we wonder if there isn't some easy way out. Some parents hope that they can strike a bargain to escape the consequences or spare their children the consequences of their actions.

I remember speaking with a woman who was strongly opposed to abortion. She marched, she wrote letters, she donated to Right to Life. But when her daughter got pregnant, she wondered if there wasn't an easier way out than having to deal with the shame and embarrassment of an unplanned grandchild. She asked the question, "Must this happen to us?" and answered it with a resounding no. Early one morning she took her daughter to the clinic and signed her up for an abortion. Her daughter, only fifteen, confused and afraid, didn't protest. She assumed her mother knew what she was doing. The next week the abortion was over and Mom's problems were over. But the daughter was troubled by bad dreams and felt so guilty that she became suicidal.

Be careful as you move through this stage. Remember that you aren't totally rational, that every idea isn't going to be a good one. Realize that actions have consequences and there is probably no way to avoid them. And know that operating contrary to your values and your morality will affect you down the line. It is impossible to do as this woman did and not struggle afterward. In our effort to strike a bargain to get our children and our families out of their problems, we cannot just look for the easy way out. We have to find the right way through.

This Really Is Happening to Us!

Reality can only be denied, questioned, and bargained over for so long. Eventually we have to face the fact this is really happening to our family. *Yes, our son really is on drugs. We can't hide it anymore. Or yes, our daughter is living with her boyfriend. There is no denying the truth.* With this sense of reality comes a sense of impending doom. We feel like the world is going to stop spinning on its axis and that the sky is going to cave in on us. The reality when our fears come true is tough to deal with, and we have to sort out blame at this stage. *Whose fault is this really? Is it mine? Is it my child's? Is it the way I was raised? Is it the school's fault?* We begin to cast around desperately looking for someone to pin the responsibility on.

There is a very real possibility that we will find a scapegoat and heap the blame on him or her. As I came to grips with my brother's life-dominating mistake and moved through this phase, I wanted it to be Lynette's fault. I wanted to put all the blame on her and excuse my brother. After all, my brother was only human, I reasoned. He probably had been enticed into this. The reality that there was enough blame to go around for everyone didn't matter. I wanted it to be someone's fault, and because of my loyalty to my brother, I felt that it couldn't be his.

Our loyalties can become very confused during times of family crisis. We want to absolve our own flesh and blood from blame, but inside we know that isn't fair. That creates anger and frustration that can come out in violent mood swings, words of hurt and pain directed at others in our family, or anger at ourselves. As we deal with the reality that this is happening to us, we must resist the urge to fix blame on someone or something. We must be careful that our sense of impending doom and dread doesn't influence what we say and do too much. There is a very real possibility that at this phase we will say something we will regret the rest of our lives.

Ernie was a good father. He loved his kids and his wife and had great plans for their futures. When his son was caught snorting cocaine with two of his friends in the locker room, Ernie came unglued. He couldn't believe that this was happening to him. He had tried so hard to protect his kids from this kind of stuff and now his son was suspended from school and in trouble with the law.

As Ernie worked his way through the stages of loss, he finally realized that this *was* happening to his family and that it *was* his son's fault. Ernie walked into his son's bedroom and threw all of his clothes into a big suitcase. He then marched into the living room and told his son that he was no longer welcome in the house. His son cried and begged him to let him stay, but it was to no avail. Ernie had decided that his family's problems were caused by his son and that his son was going to leave. "I don't care that you are my son. You have brought dishonor to this house. I have worked for twenty-five years to give you everything you needed, and this is the repayment I get. You are no longer my son."

Ernie's reaction may have been extreme, but when we are faced with those kinds of situations, our reactions can be extreme and we can say things that wound someone forever.

We Can Go On Even Though This Is Happening to Us

The final phase is the most important. The key to dealing with reality when our worst fears come true is to make it to this stage. We know what is happening, and we know that it is not the end of the world. Oh, it may feel like the end of the world and it may sometimes seem like everything is crashing down around us, but the truth is that our family can survive this crisis. Not only can we hang on and survive, we can even thrive—though occasional feelings of deep loss, grief, and depression may linger.

When our worst fears come true, it does feel like the world has spun out of control, like God has turned His back on us and given up. It does feel shameful and embarrassing. We are disappointed in ourselves or in our children. But the truth is that we can go on. We can continue to live our lives. Even after the death of a child, we can go on. Even when we have an unexpected grandchild, we can go on. Even when our children have renounced their faith and have disowned us, we can go on.

The key, according to family researchers, is a thing called

cohesiveness. It is a characteristic that strong families exhibit. It means that when things get tough, the family is bound together by the unbreakable, invisible threads of love, loyalty, and respect. We need to develop a sense of cohesion in our families. We need to build that unbreakable safety net of love, honor, respect, and loyalty. With that in place, we know that we can handle the inevitable difficult times.

There is another important key to handling family crises. Secular family researchers call it spiritual wellness. We know it by another name: *Christian faith*. I know that our family would not have survived that difficult summer without God. We questioned Him and we asked Him to get rid of the situation. We even blamed Him for the problem. But underneath it all, we realized that He is God and we are not. We knew that He loved us and could see us through. Without Him we wouldn't have had anywhere to turn.

Our story of family fears has a happy ending. My brother has been married to Lynette for nine years. They have a great marriage and two wonderful kids. He and Lynn weighed their choices, and after an entire summer of pondering, they were married. My brother even finished college and is now an engineer.

Through our story we learned two very important things. The first we have already mentioned. When it feels like the world is coming to an end, it probably isn't. What seems enormous now will not look so big in hindsight. You can make it through.

The second thing we learned was that during times of family crisis we feel alone and bereft of friends. But the truth is that we are not alone. There are others who want to care for you and your family. They want to help. They are just waiting for you to ask. There are professionals who can help you work through your disappointment and anger, your sense of betrayal and shame. They are just waiting for a phone call. And, of course, in the best way possible you are not alone. God cares. He has walked the lonely road of giving up His Son. He knows your fears, and He is there.

Our story had a happy ending. Not every story does. But a happy ending isn't necessarily one where people solve their problems without struggle. Your family fears can have a happy ending if your family grows through the struggle. If you survive as a family unit, perhaps even grow closer, building your cohesiveness and your relationship with God, you have done very well.

Stay with us now through Part Three of *Family Fears* as we unravel the mystery of how to overcome the worries that threaten our families.

Overcoming Our Fears

CHAPTER NINE

Acknowledging Our Fears

Donna looked around her bedroom walls searching for answers. She was awake again at 3:30 A.M., unable to sleep, worried about her oldest daughter. Kim wasn't home from her date, and Donna's imagination was running wild. She was convinced that her daughter was having sex with her boyfriend. She just had a feeling, just kind of knew inside her heart that it was true. But she was afraid to talk to Kim about it. Donna told herself that Kim would just lie to her anyway, so why bother? She wondered what had gone wrong with her daughter. She wondered how she had failed Kim, what she could have done differently as a parent.

The minutes dragged on and Donna's imagination was fertile. *Maybe she's been hurt, maybe she's run away. Maybe she's moved in with him. Maybe I'll never see her again.* Then Donna heard the sound of a car in the driveway, a door opening and closing. Donna got out of bed, grabbed her old robe, and met her daughter coming up the stairs.

"Kim, what happened? Why are you home so late?"

"Time just got away from us, Mom. I'm tired. See ya in the morning." Kim went into her bedroom and closed the door. Donna stayed in the hall, wondering what she should do, wondering what she *could* do.

Her fears for her daughter were ruining her life. She knew that her husband was frustrated with her about this. She was frustrated with herself, but she was paralyzed by her fear. She went back to bed, pulled up the covers, and had just about drifted off to sleep when her husband rolled over and said: "Donna, you've got to stop torturing yourself. You can't control what Kim does outside of this house. Your fear is driving me crazy." Donna knew that she was afraid, but it didn't seem right to tell anyone else. After all, she was a Christian and Christians were supposed to trust God. They weren't supposed to lie awake at night with worry. Her friends would think that she wasn't a good Christian, and if they even guessed at her fears about her daughter, Kim would be looked down on in church. Who could she turn to? Donna knew that her fear was eating her up inside, that it was time to break the silence, time to get some help.

Two days later Donna called her friend Brenda and they spent some time together over lunch. Donna gathered up all of the courage she could find and blurted out to Brenda that she was afraid that Kim was sleeping with her boyfriend and that she was going to ruin her life. She then waited for Brenda to tell her how foolish she was and to lecture her about trusting God.

But Brenda did neither of those things. Instead she leaned forward, grabbed Donna's hand, and said, "You know what? When Kyle was in college, we worried about him a lot too. I thought that he was going to turn completely away from God and church. I worried that he would really make a mess of his life. My fear got so strong that it almost completely controlled me. But I saw a counselor, and I felt so different after I admitted that I was afraid. It was like a load off of my back."

Donna nodded in amazement. She couldn't believe that perfect Brenda had been as afraid as she was. She couldn't believe that she wasn't the only person paralyzed by fear. Mostly, Donna couldn't believe how good it felt to let someone in on her fears, to share the load with another person.

The first step in overcoming our family fears is to admit

that we are afraid. That sounds like simplistic advice, but it is very important. We have to be honest with ourselves and with our families, admitting, "I am afraid. And my fear is at least partially controlling me." Unless we do this, we cannot ever really deal with the fear itself. Many of us live our lives denying that fear is a motivator in our lives. We deny that it affects our parenting and our marriages. We deny that our fear controls us and causes us to overreact. We don't want to admit that we are afraid, that family fears are influencing us.

Our refusal to admit our fear is caused by a myriad of different things. First and foremost, however, I think that our inability to admit and recognize our fear comes from shame. We are ashamed that our fears are out of hand. We are ashamed that we haven't trusted God enough or trusted our own families enough to overcome these fears. The fact of the matter is that without admitting that we are afraid, without owning up to the fact that fear is a motivator in our lives, we will not be able to deal with our fears and they will get worse, not better.

Why Is It So Crucial to Admit Our Fears?

It can be especially difficult for us to admit that we are influenced by fears because Christians aren't supposed to be afraid. We are supposed to be fearless, trusting God to provide. Admitting that we are afraid feels like failure and spiritual failure at that. We feel like others will look down on us for not being strong enough Christians to handle these fears on our own. We are sure that God is disappointed with us.

That is faulty thinking, the kind that feeds the growth of our fears and keeps us from getting them under control. It is natural and normal to fear, natural and normal to worry about our children. It is also common for these fears to grow and become problematic. It isn't a sin to be afraid. It is sin to let our fears consume us and destroy our families, instead of admitting and recognizing we are afraid and we need help.

It is absolutely vital we admit our fears. Denial means fear will continue to plague us and our families. Denial means the fear will grow in its control over us. Denial means we will stand by and let our lives be ruined by the nameless ominous sense of dread that pervades our families.

There are three reasons why we deny we are afraid. *First,* we have not had role models show us it is okay to admit to our fear. Many of us grew up in homes where males were taught not to show fear, and that being afraid was not a masculine quality. Instead we subconsciously learn to deny fear. We pretend that it is not there, that it does not exist, even though it is tearing us apart inside.

Phil was a successful forty-year-old businessman with a beautiful home and a wonderful family. If a person were to look at Phil, he would never know the fear that consumes him. He would never know that Phil lays awake at night unable to sleep and wakes up in the morning fearful that his daughter is going to come downstairs and give him the news that she has made a life-dominating mistake. A person would never know that when Phil goes to work all he can think about on the commute is that his son will come home with the news that he had been suspended from school or from the football team.

Phil has become very good at covering up his fears, of denying they exist. Phil's father had told him many years ago that real men aren't afraid, and followed that up by saying Christians don't have to be afraid. They can just trust God. The message that Phil got was simple. If you are serious about your Christianity and if you are a man, you are never afraid. And so instead of dealing with his fear, instead of admitting he is afraid, and taking that first step toward healing, Phil continues to deny that he is afraid. He pushes it down. He represses it. And as the fear grows, it grows into control, into a destructive power wreaking havoc on his family.

The *second* reason we deny our fear is a pseudo-spirituality. Many of us have grown up in homes that say emotions are bad, that we shouldn't feel afraid. The truth is the Bible is full of people who owned up to their fears. True spirituality is not an absence of fear. It is taking your fear to God and giving it to Him. It is not denying you are afraid. It is using the power of the Holy Spirit in your life to work through your fear and to do the right thing even though you are afraid. The Apostle Paul himself said, "I came to you in weakness and fear, and with much trembling" (1 Corinthians 2:3). All of us are afraid. All of us struggle with fear taking control of our lives. It is not unchristian, or unspiritual, or sinful, or evil to be afraid. But we *can* become sinful in the way that we handle our fears.

Perhaps, the really sinful way of handling our fears is to deny them all the while they are growing, influencing our families and moving us away from God. True spirituality says, "I am afraid. I worry about my family. My fear is controlling me sometimes. It is changing the way I parent." True spirituality is taking that fear and giving it to God. We will talk about this more in a later chapter.

The *third* reason that we deny our fears is that we do not want to admit weakness. Fear feels like weakness. This is especially true for men. We have been brought up to believe that fear is synonymous with weakness. It shows that somehow we are not true men, that we are not strong enough to handle the relationships and problems that arise in our lives. The truth of the matter, of course, is that we have to admit that we are afraid in order to deal with it. One cannot deal with a problem that does not exist. Until we admit to ourselves that we are afraid, we will never be able to take the steps necessary to bring our fear under control, to take away its power, to keep it from dominating our lives.

Naming the Fear Takes Away Its Power

The second reason that we need to admit our fears is because naming the fear takes away its power. The nameless unspeakable dread that we carry around gnaws at us all the time. It weighs on our minds during our waking and sleeping hours alike. We carry it like a lead weight on our backs, a burden to be borne. It nurtures more fear and creates a malaise of the spirit.

How do we name our fears? We need to be specific. We

need to say, "I am afraid of my child's budding sexuality." And maybe even take it a bit further, perhaps, "I am afraid of my child becoming pregnant." Now that we have identified this specific fear, we need to examine it, asking ourselves, "Why am I afraid? What are the consequences?" We need to get a clear picture of our fear and what it entails.

To illustrate this, let me tell you a story about something that happened in our house not too long ago. One evening my children, Erin and Jonathon, had punched a hole in a screen on one of our doors, not a very big hole, about two inches around. We were unable to get the screen fixed that night but did not think much about it as the weather was warm and there weren't many bugs. While we were out that night, a bat pushed its way through that hole into our house.

After we had been home for about an hour, getting everyone ready for bed, Leslie, my wife, ran upstairs, grabbed me by the arm and pulled me downstairs to the dining room. She pointed up to the corner. And there, up near the ceiling, sleeping peacefully, was a bat. I was terrified, but being a man, I knew it was my responsibility to "evict" the creature. So I grabbed a broom, sent my wife and kids into a bedroom, and went after the bat. I took one swing at Mr. Bat and managed to hit it. I hit it just enough to wake it from its peaceful slumber and send it circling again and again around the light and my head in the dining room.

Now my fear had complete control of me. I ran into the bedroom with my wife and kids. And there we sat, huddled around each other, wondering what we were going to do. By now it was late and way past the kids' bedtime. Being the red-blooded American male, I did the right thing. I offered to sleep in that bedroom, on that floor, with the whole family for the night. We decided to worry about the bat the next day.

The next day dawned, and with it my courage returned. I went on a bat hunt. Unfortunately, the bat was nowhere to be found. I chose to believe that the bat had disappeared. Because I had chosen to deny my fear in the light of day, and because I could not see it, I believed that it had gone away. I informed my family that the bat was gone and that I had taken care of the problem, and we went about our business. Until that night.

At 11:30, while sitting around our living room chatting with our good friends, John and Julie, our bat made a return appearance. It came flying out of the kitchen, through the dining room and into the living room. As it swooped low over us, we all dove to the floor in fear and began throwing decorative pillows and anything else within reach at the encircling creature.

Eventually, the bat flew up the stairs and into our daughter's bedroom. Fortunately Erin and Jonathon were asleep on the floor of Jonathon's room, still scared about the previous evening's episode with the bat. John and I stood next to the bedroom, broom in hand, and cautiously shut the door, knowing that the bat was inside. We stood outside the door discussing our options. There were only two that we could see. We could leave the bat in Jonathon's room for the night, once again hoping that the bat would somehow disappear, or we could go in and face the bat.

After much discussion, we decided to go in. Perhaps each of us was worried about what the other would think if we admitted that we were too afraid to go. So, armed with a broom and a blanket, we walked in and stalked the bat. We looked under the bed, behind the dresser, and behind the blinds on the windows. Once again we believed that the bat had disappeared. As a last resort we kicked a plastic toy bin full of toys and out flew the bat.

In this room with very low ceilings we began to yell as once again our fear gained control of us. I threw the blanket, hoping to capture the bat. I did hit the bat with the blanket and it flew dazed at John who knocked it up against a wall with the broom and killed it. As the bat lay there on the floor and we stood breathing heavily, trying to conquer the fear and the adrenaline that was coursing through our bodies, we walked over to examine our victim. When we looked at it, our fears seemed pretty irrational because this bat was small, no bigger than a very small mouse. Its wing span had seemed large, but it obviously was not big enough to cause us any harm. I realized that this bat had probably been as afraid of me as I had been of it. The fear had caused me to be act very irrationally and to run away and hide.

Fear in our lives is like that. Most of us, when confronted by a fear, run and hide in the bedroom. We shut the door. We block out the fear for as long as we can, and we hope it is gone and won't come back. When we wake up in the morning, we no longer feel the fear. We kid ourselves into believing it is gone and will never make a return appearance. However, the fear inevitably comes back when things take a downward turn. It comes back with more power than ever before.

Naming the fear is just like looking at the bat. We realize that it is not going to take away everything that we hold dear. We examine and see what it really is, instead of letting it be a nameless powerful force that haunts our waking and sleeping hours. As we examine our fear, turn it around, and name it specifically, it becomes more clear what we are up against. Then we can begin to deal with it in a rational way, focusing on the root of our often bizarre actions and feelings. If we don't take this important step, the fear will grow in its power and destructiveness in our family relationships.

Admitting and naming our fear is a four-step process. The first step is to *look at ourselves and our actions very honestly.* This is difficult because it involves stripping away the veneer and the walls we have built to keep us from admitting the fact that we are afraid. But we need to look deep inside, into the dark crevasses of our soul where we don't often go and determine how much of an influence fear is having on us. Is fear in control of our discipline? Is fear the reason we have grounded our son? Is fear the reason we push our children harder and harder, driving them on to success, pushing them to achieve? Is it fear behind the outbursts of anger, the impatience? Honestly and truthfully, how much influence is fear having on our lives?

We need to look for the "reason behind the reason." You

may think that your family is struggling because you are so angry. Perhaps you need to look at why you are so angry. Is it fear? Is it the fear your children are not going to "turn out right," that they will not live out your values? Is fear driving your anger? You need to stare into the darkness that lies within and be honest with yourself as you search for the fear you don't want to name or admit. You need to admit it. You need to name it and acknowledge that it is controlling your actions and changing the way you parent.

The second way we admit our fear is to *realize it is okay to be afraid.* Being afraid is not a sin. The emotion of fear is not sinful. It is what we do with that emotion, the way that we act on it, or whether we let it take root that determines whether or not it is sinful. Fear is a natural response to external stimuli. When we are confronted with situations we don't know how to handle, fear pops up. When we look at our children and see how the decisions they are making now could affect their lives forever, fear is a natural result. It is not sinful to be afraid.

It is sinful to deny the fear, to let it take root, to let it control our actions, to allow it to dominate our family dynamics. Often our guilt at being afraid keeps us from admitting it. In order to admit our fear we need to realize that it is okay to be afraid. It is okay to look at our children and wonder and worry. It is okay to wonder if we are failing. It is okay to fear that our children are not going to live out our values. It is okay to be afraid.

The third step to admitting our fear is to *tell others about our fear, to share our load.* Galatians 6:2 tells us to "carry each other's burdens, and in this way . . . fulfill the law of Christ." The Greek word for *burden* means a load that is too big for one person to carry alone. The Bible calls for fellow believers to come alongside those who are carrying a burden that is too big for them to bear. If fear is a burden that is too big for you, you must turn to someone you trust and love and admit to them that you are afraid. You must share your load of fear with them so that together the two or three or four of you can distribute the load, and you can make it.

Sixteen-year-old Rex looked at his family and saw that things were not going well. Although both of his parents were Christians, it was obvious they were not getting along. They did not speak to each other much, and a tension reigned in the house whenever they were both present. Rex wondered and worried how long his family would stay together. In fact, it became an all-consuming fear that dominated his life. He became worried that every time he did something wrong he was contributing to the tension. He began to feel that it was his responsibility to hold the family together.

The burden of fear grew and grew until he could no longer bear the weight of his burden. But Rex did what many adults don't do. He went to a friend. He went to an adult friend, his youth pastor from church, and said, "I am afraid, and I can't bear this alone anymore. Will you help me?" Adults too need to turn to a trusted friend, to a pastor, to a spouse and say, "I am afraid, and the burden has grown too big for me, and I can no longer bear it alone. Will you take some of this load and help me bear this burden and so fulfill the law of Christ?"

Finally, and most importantly, we need to tell God about our fears. When David wrote Psalm 142, he was in a cave running from Saul who was trying to kill him. Listen to David's words:

> I cry aloud to the Lord; I lift up my voice to the Lord for mercy. I pour out my complaint before Him. Before Him I tell my trouble. When my spirit grows faint within me, it is You who know my way. In the path where I walk men have hidden a snare for me. Look to my right and see; no one is concerned for me. I have no refuge; no one cares for my life. I cry to You, O Lord; I say, "You are my refuge, my portion in the land of the living." Listen to my cry for I am in desperate need; rescue me from those who pursue me, for they are too strong for me. Set me free from my prison, that I may praise Your name. Then the righteous will gather about me because of Your goodness to me.

If David, who was called a man after God's own heart, who was certainly one of the most courageous men who ever lived, a man who fought wild animals, a man who was renowned for his battle skills, if David would turn in the midst of his fear and cry out to God for help, certainly you and I can do the same. To admit our fear we need to look to God and say, "I cannot handle this fear on my own. I cry out to You, God." We need to take the fear that is controlling us, that is dominating our lives, the nameless dread that is at the back of our minds, and we need to deposit it at the feet of Jesus. We need to say to Him, "Here is my burden, Lord. I cannot handle it without You."

God will not let you walk alone. He will pick you up, dust you off, and send you back on your way when you fall. God says, "When you are afraid, I will be with you. When you feel alone in the dark and the fear is consuming you, I will be with you there. When you look at your family and wonder if it really is going to be all right, I am there. When you look at your husband and wonder if he is faithful, I am there. When you look at your children and wonder if they will follow Me, I am there. I am the God of Abraham, Isaac, and Jacob, and I am your God as well."

■　　　■　　　■

The keys then to admitting our fears are simple. We need to look at ourselves and our actions honestly, being realistic about how fear is controlling us. We need to realize that it is okay to be afraid. We need to accept that being afraid, the emotion, is not sin. What we do with that emotion and how we act on it and whether or not we allow it to take root and control our lives determines if we are in sin or not. We need to tell others about our fear, to share our load as the Bible tells us, and finally we need to tell God. God has promised He will not give us any load that is too heavy to bear, and He will never let us walk alone. We are His children. He will always be near to us, and He has promised to take our fear when we look to Him and admit that we are afraid and need His help.

When seeking to gain knowledge and understanding of our fear, we need to determine whether our fear is rational or irrational. We do that by asking ourselves questions about our feelings. For example, if you are afraid that your child is abusing alcohol, you need to find out why you are feeling that way. What is the evidence that your child is drinking? Have you caught him coming home drunk? Has the quality of his schoolwork dropped precipitously? Is he hanging around a different group of friends? Have you found alcohol in his room? Have you smelled it on his breath?

Or do you just have a vague feeling of unease, a worry in the back of your mind that your son is drinking? Is it family history that is concerning you? Or perhaps you have a close friend whose child is abusing alcohol? Finding a can of beer in your son's room may not be a sign of alcoholism, but it certainly warrants an explanation. On the other hand, a vague feeling isn't enough evidence on which to base an accusation.

Another way to help understand whether our fear is rational or irrational is by paying attention to how much we are thinking about the fear. We asked one father to write down every time he worried about how his son was going to turn out. To be honest, we anticipated about ten times a day, which would have been a substantial amount. Instead, when he honestly wrote down every time he felt a stab of fear for his son, he totalled over fifty times a day!

Do you visualize your fear as having taken place? Can you see it in your mind's eye? Is it a general fear: "I hope my kid doesn't get mixed up in drugs"? Or is it more specific, "I hope my daughter isn't smoking pot with her friend Ben"? Are your work or other relationships affected by this fear? Are you functioning normally or are you extremely irritable, close to tears, or angry under the surface?

After answering these questions, it is time to assess the risk factor. If your fear becomes reality, what are the consequences for your child or your family? What is the worst-case scenario? What is the most probable outcome?

Take a look at the probability. How possible is this event? Almost anything can happen, but it usually doesn't. Most of the time people act like they have for years. If you are afraid that your wife is having an affair, you need to ask yourself if that would be out of character for her. Is she really capable of deceiving you? Would she do it if she had the chance? We need to look at the big picture of life. Does this action fit this person?

When we are gripped by fear, it can be very difficult to see the big picture. We become obsessed with the fear. We are focused on it and it alone. This narrow perspective prevents us from really assessing the risk factor. When we are obsessed, the most unlikely events seem probable. Are you focused on the fear to such a degree that you are failing to see the good things happening in your family, with your children, or your spouse?

In order to help determine whether your fear is rational or irrational, we have put together a short self-test found on the next page. Take it and help assess the risk in your family.

Chapter Checklist

Complete the following checklist and talk about it with your family. Use this scale to answer each statement. Circle the number which best represents your answer.

1 = Strongly Agree, 2 = Agree, 3 = Undecided,
4 = Disagree, 5 = Strongly Disagree

1 2 3 4 5   1. My fears are based on objective, observable facts.

1 2 3 4 5   2. I can think about my fears without panicking.

1 2 3 4 5   3. I can easily admit that I am afraid.

1 2 3 4 5   4. I have named my specific fears.

1 2 3 4 5   5. I have shared my fears with others.

1 2 3 4 5   6. I have assessed the risk factor in my fears.

1 2 3 4 5   7. I seldom think that the very worst will happen.

1 2 3 4 5   8. I seldom lose any sleep thinking about one or more of my fears.

1 2 3 4 5   9. I think that even if some of my worst fears do come true it would not be the end of the world. I could go on with my life.

1 2 3 4 5   10. Often personal growth comes through difficult times and circumstances.

Scoring: If you scored less than 25, you are very realistic and readily admit your fears. A score between 25 and 35 indicates that you are somewhat uncertain about how well you are doing. You may need some encouragement. If you scored over 35, you may need some help in assessing and dealing with your fears.

CHAPTER TEN

Managing Our Fear

J anet looked anxiously around the well-appointed recep-
tion area, wondering if the other people waiting for ap-
pointments were also making their first trip to a psychologist. *Did they think that she was crazy? Did they look at her
and wonder whether she had lost it completely?* After all, if
you would have asked Janet just a few short months ago
whether she would ever have needed to see a therapist, she
would have laughed in your face. Her life was going along
fine, thank you. Her husband seemed happy, their home was
paid for, and their youngest daughter was going off to college.
Janet was looking forward to having more time for herself and
spending less time worrying about her children. She looked
back over her life and considered herself a good parent, who
had done the right things and had turned out good kids.

At least that was how she had felt then. But everything
hadn't turned out as Janet planned. As matter of fact, Janet
was in the counselor's office waiting to find out how she could
regain control of a life that had seemingly spun out of control.

It had started coming undone with her daughter's announcement that she was not attending Bible college. As a
matter of fact, she was not attending college at all. It seems
that Janet's daughter had met a man, and they were in love,

and she was moving in with him. She said that she would get a job and things would all work out.

"You'll see, Mom," she said. "I know that you are upset now, but you will see that this is really what I need to do for me. I don't feel the same way about things that you do, and maybe I never have. I love Dave, and he loves me, and we will be very happy. I had hoped that you would be happy for us."

The words had shocked Janet into the reality that her daughter, the perfect Christian child, was not who Janet had thought she was. Listening to her daughter's words, repudiating everything that she held dear, was almost too much for her to bear. Her husband characteristically ignored the situation and pretended that it did not exist, and the weight of handling it, explaining to her friends what had happened to her daughter, the load of guilt and shame, fell squarely on Janet's shoulders.

At first it had been difficult for Janet to go back to church because every time she walked in she knew that everyone was thinking that she had failed as a parent and that somehow along the way she had not been a good enough Christian. She hadn't prayed enough or had not read the Bible enough with her daughter, and that was why her daughter had turned her back on the faith and moved in with this guy.

But it was worse than that. Her daughter had turned her back not only on her faith but also on all their values about education, career, and her future. Her daughter had repudiated all of them.

As Janet watched her daughter carry her bags to the car, she was struck by a sudden stab of fear that she would never see her daughter again, or that if she did, their relationship would never be the same. Janet had run out of the house crying, embarrassing herself with the rawness of her emotion. She pulled on her daughter's sleeve and was shaken off like a horse shaking off a fly.

Her daughter had finally said, "Mother, leave me alone. I have to make my own choices. I will call you."

Then the waiting began. Six weeks went by without a word.

Janet did not know where her daughter was, where she was living, how she was surviving. She had no clue as to her daughter's welfare. Then came the phone call she had been waiting for.

"Hi Mom! It's Allison. I'm doing all right. Don't worry about me. I will be fine." Then, a click. No time for questions, no time to find out what was really happening. But those questions haunted Janet anyway—every single night as sleep stayed far away and she wondered how she had failed as a parent. She wondered what would happen to Allison. Most importantly and vividly, she was haunted by the fear that her daughter would not come back to Christ. She couldn't get rid of this nagging feeling in the back of her mind that her daughter was going to hell. She did not want to think about hell, a place she could not associate with her daughter's eternal fate.

Janet had gone to her pastor for help, and although well meaning, his platitudes and prayers fell on deaf ears. They could not cover the hurt and increasingly the fear that was growing inside of Janet. She tried to talk to her husband about it, but once again, he did not understand why she was so afraid and why this was such a problem. He simply said, "Our daughter is a grown woman. She is going to make her own choices. What are you so worried about?"

Yet every day the fear grew that her daughter was making a mistake that would ruin her life, that she would not turn out right, and even more that she would forever reject her parents' values.

It had finally come to this point. Janet was sitting in a psychologist's waiting room trying to find a way out of the depths of depression, trying to find a way past the anger and frustration that seemed to grip her daily. As she walked into the counselor's office, she wondered if he would understand. She wondered if he would really be able to help her.

It did not take long before Janet knew that she had come to the right place. Her psychologist did not seem like a psychologist at all. He wore a polo shirt and jeans. He seemed relaxed and didn't have a couch. He asked her one simple question,

"Janet, what are you most afraid of?"

Out poured all kinds of answers. "I'm afraid that Allison is going to get pregnant, that she will get a disease. I am afraid that he is going to abandon her. I am afraid that she is never going to come back to Jesus. I am afraid that she is going to embarrass and bring shame to our family. I am afraid that she is going to make the kind of mistake that will stay with her forever. I am afraid that she is never going to get an education. I am afraid. . . . "

He stopped her gently with a touch of his hand on her arm saying, "Janet, I asked you what you are most afraid of."

"I don't know," she replied. "I am just so afraid all the time that it has become overwhelming."

Janet's counselor asked a second question, "What can you do about what your daughter is doing?"

"I don't know," Janet admitted. "Maybe I could go and find her and beg her to come back, talk to her and convince her that she is really better off at home and with us than with him."

The counselor shook his head gently. "What can you do really? How can you deal with this fear?"

In chapter nine we talked about the importance of admitting and understanding our fears. If we don't admit our fears, they don't really exist for us and we can't really deal with them. We talked about understanding our fear, deciding whether or not our fear was rational or irrational, assessing the risk and the probability of our fears coming to pass. In this chapter, we are going to take a look at the next step. Many of us stop at admitting and understanding our fears. We come to that point and then turn around and refuse to deal with them.

This chapter is about dealing with our fears. It is about doing what we can do instead of worrying about what we can't do. Dealing with our fears is really a six-step process.

Step #1: Acknowledge Your Limitations

It is very difficult for us to understand that we cannot make other people do what we want them to do. We cannot force them to act in ways that we want them to act. With our small children, of course, because we are bigger and because we are their parents, we can force them to act the way we want them to act when they are with us. But even small children, as anyone who is a parent will know, will do as they please when they are away from their parents.

Teenagers are the same way. Often when our teenager is out on a date, we wonder if he or she is acting in ways that we consider acceptable. And we would like to reach out to them on that date and control everything that they do, but we cannot do this. It is impossible. We cannot really control others. We talked earlier in the book about how this inevitably results in frustration. The control slips through our fingers when our children or our husband or wife refuse to respond to our attempts to control. Sometimes the very one we seek to control responds negatively to our control and pushes farther away. Out of that frustration and lack of control comes anger, and out of anger comes emotional or physical distance and once again comes fear.

It is very difficult to say, "I really can't do anything about this situation." It has been said that love covers a multitude of sins, and this is true. But love cannot undo what has been done, and love cannot take away the consequences of bad choices. As parents we often think that with love and concern we can make everything that is bad good. We think that just as when our children were small, we can kiss away all the hurt and the pain. The fact is that as our children grow, we can no longer kiss away all the hurt and pain. The choices that they make, the choices that our husbands and our wives make, result often in hurt or pain that will not easily go away.

Acknowledging our limitations is important because it reduces our responsibility. When we are always trying to take control of the situation, always trying to make our spouse's or our children's mistakes right, what we do is we take responsibility for their actions. And then they are free, of course, to keep on making mistakes. When we realize our limitations, we refuse the responsibility that does not belong to us, and we put it back where it belongs, on our children, our wife, or husband.

This is hard for many of us to do because we have grown to like all that responsibility. It meets our need for power, and we have come to like being depended on. But this is not healthy. It is not right. What happens is that we carry around guilt that is not ours. We spend our time worrying about situations that we really can't control. We feel like we are to blame when things go wrong. Acknowledging our limitations, what we can and cannot do, releases us from this unnecessary guilt and this burden of shame.

Step #2: Recognize Your Capabilities

As we speak to families about family fears, and as we counsel them and help them to see how fear is influencing their lives, one of the things that constantly surprises us is how insecure parents are about their parenting abilities. In order to deal with our fears, we need to recognize that we are doing all we can do. But all we can do is usually enough. Many of us have spent a lot of time agonizing over the bad choices that we have made as parents. It is time for us to look back over our lives and to realize, to recognize, what we have done right.

In our culture, parents take the blame for everything for their children, from poor self-esteem to prison sentences. But the fact of the matter is that our children are responsible for their choices just as we are responsible for our choices. When we recognize our capabilities, we look back over our lives and we say, "I have done the best that I can do. Maybe I wasn't prepared to be a parent. Maybe I wasn't emotionally mature enough to be a parent. Maybe I made some mistakes along the way, but I have done the best that I can do and I have loved with everything that is in my soul. And I have done my best to show that love and to spread that love to my children."

A mother was sitting in my father's office, her head in her hands. She looked up at my father and said, "Do you ever think that some people were just never meant to be parents?"

My dad smiled and said, "I have felt like that often too, but what makes you think that?"

She went on to relate some of the things that she had said to her son, some of the actions she had taken, some of the choices and mistakes that she had made.

At the end of her litany of woe, Dad looked at her and said, "You are a good parent. When I listen to the choices that you have made, the way you have disciplined, and the way you are handling your son, all I can say is I couldn't have done better myself and I think you are doing a great job."

Her eyes opened wide in amazement. "But what about all my mistakes?"

"Hey, everybody makes mistakes," Dad said. "I could spend a lifetime telling you about mine. You have surrounded your child with a loving and caring environment, and that is an enormous thing to do."

This woman is a good parent, but she cannot see it. She will not admit that she is doing the best that she can do. She does not recognize her capabilities. And it is keeping her from dealing with her fear, because every time she thinks about the things that scare or worry her, it always comes back to, "Whatever he is doing, it must be my fault because I have been a bad parent." Her fear is gaining control of her largely because she does not realize how good a mother she really is.

Step #3: Believe in Your Family

If you believe in your family, you can have some confidence that your children will surprise you with the good choices that they make. Your kids are all right. Give them time.

I spend much of my time speaking to high-school and junior-high students. Often I spend time with them before and after I speak. I enjoy being with them and hearing their stories, but the one thing that always surprises me is how different high-school and junior-high school students are from their stereotypes. They are much more concerned, caring, loving, and decent than they are given credit for. I am impressed with the quality of teenagers in America. I think they are terrific people. I think if you take an honest look at your kids, you will see that they are terrific people as well. In our culture we focus on the negative with teenagers. Every time we turn on the television there is a teenager in the news accused of some heinous crime. Every time we watch a movie about teenagers we see them drinking, having sex, or doing things that put fear in our hearts when we think about our own teenagers. Many teenagers are not involved in those kinds of activities; many are making good choices.

Even if your teenager is making bad choices right now, there is hope. We have often seen in our work with families that those who have made bad choices and then continue to make bad choices, at some point stop, turn around, and come back. We have seen students who totally rejected Christianity at eighteen and now at twenty-nine are sitting in church every Sunday singing the hymns. They realized that they were wrong and had turned around and come back to the faith. Your children may need to travel this road too.

When you look at your family and all you see is failure because you are not living up to some invisible standard of what a Christian family ought to be, try looking instead at what your family is doing right.

First, *focus on the positive.* Pick out the things that you are doing right as a family. Think about the times when you have been together as a family and just had an incredibly good time. Think about the things that you have done as a family that you are proud of. Think about the things that your children have done that you are proud of. Think about the things your husband or wife has done that you are proud of. Focus on the positive.

As a high-school student I did not care as much for my studies as my parents wanted me to, and I am sure they often worried about my lack of diligence. They wondered if I would ever get serious. One semester I came home with a report card containing five "A's" and one "D." I was fairly proud of the five A's and I thought that I would be able to slide with the one D because the A's would make up for it. I was wrong.

When I walked into the house, my parents quickly scanned the report card, taking the five A's in stride. After all, they expected A's from their son. But when they got to the D, they went ballistic. "How could you get a D? What were you thinking? Didn't you care? Didn't you do your homework? You are too smart to get a D. Jack, you're grounded!" I didn't think this punishment was fair, and in very strenuous and in somewhat less than respectful tones, I let them know it, which only resulted in my grounding being lengthened.

I was resigned to my fate and went to my room to ponder the injustice of being a teenager in my family when I heard a knock on the door. My mom asked to come in.

"Yeah, what do you want?"

She responded, "Jack, I don't think we have been quite fair with you. We do not want to see D's on your report card, but those five A's are outstanding. And we are proud of you. The only reason that we are so disappointed with the D is that it contrasts so sharply with the A's. But we need to tell you that you are not grounded and that we were wrong in focusing on the only negative thing on your report card."

Can you imagine how this made me feel? All of a sudden I thought my parents understood me. I felt like maybe they realized what it was like to be a teenager, and it felt good.

How often in your family do you focus on the one D and let the five A's go by unnoticed? How often do you take for granted that you are doing well as a family? But when you have one failure, however small, it grows in importance until it blocks out your view of everything that you are doing right.

The second action we can take in order to believe in our family is to *reframe the negative*. We need to look at the negative situations, behaviors, or qualities, and put them in another context. For example, when you look at your family, you may see a lack of planning for family times together. You may think your family hasn't taken the time necessary to sit down and decide what to do for your family vacation this year. You may have read that this is what families who care about each other are supposed to do, so you have a sense that you are failing because you are not living up to this expectation.

But maybe your family just takes off sporadically to go to the movies, or takes off on the spur of the moment to go out to dinner together. So instead of saying that you don't plan well, you should say "Our family does spontaneous, impulsive, fun things together." Doesn't this feel better than dwelling on your lack of planning? Does this sound like a successful, healthy family?

When you see qualities in your children that you are not entirely satisfied or thrilled with, you can look at them and say, "Boy, my child is stubborn. He won't listen to me and he does his own thing." If you can reframe stubborn, your child becomes "determined." You can say, "My child just won't follow the rules. No matter what is laid out for him at school or at home, he always finds some way around them." Or you can say, "My child is innovative and creative."

One family I know really struggled with believing in themselves. The father especially felt that he was not what a Christian father was supposed to be. When he was reminded of all of the things they were doing right, it did not seem to mean much to him compared to the things they were doing "wrong." So his wife took it upon herself to help him see the positive. She began to post notes throughout the house that said things like, "I really enjoyed it when we were out last week. Thanks for being a great husband." The whole family caught on to the idea and began to put other notes around the house for each other. Soon the encouraging notes created a new atmosphere in their home. The family's opinion of itself began to change, and pretty soon they knew what they were doing right as a family.

Step #4: Do What You Can Do

We spend a lot of time talking about the things we cannot do as a family, actions of others which we cannot control, events we may not be able to influence. But there are often things we *can* do, and these we tend to forget about.

Maybe all you can do is pray for your family. Maybe your child has left home and you have lost contact with him or her. Maybe all you can do is pray, but you *can* pray.

We know a grandfather who watched his oldest grandson grow from a loving, caring twelve-year-old to a resentful, defiant eighteen-year-old. He watched his grandson deny the faith he had been brought up with, reject his family's values, and move away. He did not hear from the young man for a very long time. He didn't know what he was doing and what was going on in his life. His grandson had seemingly dropped off the face of the earth. Grandpa kept praying every day. He never forgot him, never gave up on him. Until one day, four years after his grandson had left, there was a knock at the door. There on the doorstep was his grandson. "Grandpa, I have come home. I am back to stay." Do what you can do, even if all you can do is pray.

In doing what you can do, it is important to make a plan of action. Sometimes you may need to go as far as writing it down, making a commitment, and giving it a time frame. By doing so, it becomes apparent what our limitations are. For example, consider the situation in which you are worried about your child's sexual activity. What can you do? Can you go with them on their dates? No. Can you make their sexual choices for them? No. Can you ensure that they will not make a bad decision? No. Can you talk with them about sexuality? Yes. Can you point out to them what God's plan for sexuality is? Yes. Can you tell them stories of others who have made good and bad choices regarding sexuality? Yes. Can you relate to them your own life story as it relates to sexuality? Yes.

A sample plan of action might look like this. *First,* set aside a time to talk to your child. Make an appointment with him or her, ensuring that it is a date and time that both of you can realistically meet. *Second,* make a list of the things you want to talk about. *Third,* make the meeting time and place as comfortable and as conducive to uninterrupted discussion as possible. *Fourth,* follow through with this plan, scheduling your day or week with this in mind, letting nothing come in the way of this commitment. It is as easy as this. Make a commitment with a time frame, and follow through with it. Do what you can do.

Doing what we can do always involves taking responsibility for our own actions. It may involve asking for forgiveness. It may mean going to your husband or wife and saying "I have been afraid. I have allowed this fear to take over, making me controlling and manipulative. I am sorry." It may involve going to one of your children and asking for forgiveness. In making a plan of action, the entire plan may focus on reconciliation, on trying to heal a relationship where fear, bad choices, and anger have driven a wedge. Don't be afraid to go to a person. Take the Bible's advice, and go to the one you have hurt, ask for forgiveness, and take responsibility for your actions.

Doing what we can do may not solve the problem. It may not even seem to help very much, but taking responsibility and taking action will reduce our guilt, decrease the load of worry and fear, and increase our self-esteem. We will know that we are not overreacting, overprotecting, or controlling. It is far better to take action and begin to move in the right direction than it is to sit around complaining and whining about how bad things are, wallowing in self-pity.

Step #5: Share Your Fear with Others

This step involves asking for help and giving our experiences to others. Sharing what we have learned with others may help them deal with their own fears.

A prominent Christian couple in our city struggled mightily with their teenage daughter. She rebelled against every rule. She rejected every belief and value that they held true. She did things that seemingly were designed to embarrass them. Her hair was blue and styled in a mohawk. She wore black leather and chains to church. Her parents were desperately afraid that she was going to make a complete disaster out of her life. They were worried about what others would think about them. They were concerned that she would never "turn out right," and most of all they despaired that she would never come back to Jesus.

In their fear they felt alone and unloved. They thought their church community could not help them because it was judging them so harshly. They had heard snide remarks about their parenting and the intimations that if they had only done a better job, their daughter would not be making these kinds of decisions. They knew it wasn't true, but at the same time those remarks gnawed at their souls and eventually caused them to question their parenting. They finally went so far as to join a parents' support group. There they found other parents who shared their fears, other parents who worried about the same things they worried about, others who were struggling with the same questions. By sharing their fears with others they realized that they were not alone. They were not the only people who felt like this. Theirs was not the only child who was making these kinds of choices. Their fears were not unique but were common to many families.

And although it did not take their fear away and it did not make their daughter act any differently, they did sleep better at night, knowing that they were doing what they could. Sharing their fears with others lightened their load. Eventually, as they grew to understand their daughter and as their daughter began to make some good choices, they were able to share how they had handled this most difficult of children, and others learned from them. We all need to share our fears and share what we have learned.

Step #6: Grow through Your Experiences

My dad always tells those he is counseling, "Don't waste a negative experience. Learn from it. Make yourself and others better, not bitter." As we handle our fears and bring them under control, as we realize our limitations, we recognize our capabilities. We begin to believe in our families. We are doing what we can do and share our experiences with others. Then we begin to grow. We learn from our experiences. We examine the mistakes we have made in the past, and hopefully we don't make them over again. We may find new ones to make, but we grow and learn from those as well.

Dealing with our fears is not easy. It is not easy to admit them. It is not easy to try to understand what we are afraid of, and it is especially not easy to take that next step and get into hand-to-hand combat with our fears. But if we don't deal with our fears, they will not go away. They will grow, and become more intense, more controlling, and more manipulating, until they are running and ruining our lives.

The choice is simple. We can play ostrich. We can stick our heads in the ground and pretend that we are not afraid or worried, or we can stand up straight, look at our fear, and bring it under control. We can learn to handle fear instead of letting it handle us.

Chapter Checklist

Complete the following checklist and talk about it with your family. Use this scale to answer each statement. Circle the number which best represents your answer.

1 = Strongly Agree, 2 = Agree, 3 = Undecided,
4 = Disagree, 5 = Strongly Disagree

1 2 3 4 5   1. I clearly recognize my limitations.

1 2 3 4 5   2. I have clearly identified my capabilities.

1 2 3 4 5   3. I believe in my family.

1 2 3 4 5   4. I am doing all I can do in the midst of my fears.

1 2 3 4 5   5. I have asked others for help and advice.

1 2 3 4 5   6. I am growing through my fears.

1 2 3 4 5   7. I am not assuming responsibility for things over which I have no control.

1 2 3 4 5   8. I am limiting my criticism of self.

1 2 3 4 5   9. I have outlined a plan of action to deal with my family fears.

1 2 3 4 5   10. I am focusing more on the positive than on the negative.

Scoring: If you scored 20 or less, you are dealing with your fears very well. A score between 20 and 30 indicates some uncertainty about how well you are doing. If you scored above 30, you may need some outside help to deal with some of your fears.

Finding God in the Midst of Our Fear

Ralph wearily walked into the house, let the door slam shut behind him, went up to his bedroom, and sat down on the side of his bed. He put his head in his hands and began to cry. His wife of fifteen years had just informed him that she was leaving him and that she did not want anything more to do with him or their family. Ralph couldn't really say that it had come as a complete surprise. Their marriage had not been good for quite some time, and he had known that his wife was unhappy with their relationship. They had been to see many counselors over the years; nothing had seemed to help. They just seemed to grow apart. But still the news that she had been seeing another man for two years, and was moving in with him and leaving her family behind had been a shock. It was a shock to his ordered world, his self-esteem, but most of all it sent a jolt of fear coursing through his body.

How was he going to make it? What would happen to their family? How would his three children learn to live without their mother and how would they react when they heard the news? What would others think of him and how would the people in his church treat him? There were no answers to his questions, only fear. Fear built upon fear until Ralph sat there shaking, sobbing, with his head in his hands, wondering what was going to happen to him now that his worst fears had come true.

Ralph looked up at the ceiling and called out to God, "God! Why is this happening to me? I have tried to do the right thing. I have tried to love my wife, to care for her, and to give her what she needs and wants. I have tried counseling, and I have done all that I can do. Everything is still a mess. It's not fair, and I don't think You really care about me, because if You cared, You would have answered my prayers for my marriage. If You cared, You would not have allowed this to happen to me. If You cared, this would have worked out. Why aren't You there now that I am so alone and afraid?"

The final step to overcoming our family fears is to learn how to find God in the midst of our struggle. Many of us feel like Ralph. We wonder why God has allowed bad things to happen to us. We question whether He cares about us. We wonder why our prayers have gone unanswered, and we wonder if it is because they have gone unheard. We do not understand. Our intentions were so good, and we have done all the "right" things. And yet bad things are happening to our family, our fear is growing daily, and it seems like we are completely alone. We ask, "God where are You?"

When trying to find God in the midst of our fears, three things happen. First, we wonder where God is or if He is there at all. We wonder why we feel so alone, if God is supposed to be there in our time of dire need. We wonder why we don't feel His presence and His comfort that everyone talks about so much. God's love seems so foreign and alien to us as we struggle with our family problems.

We need to know that it is okay to wonder where God is. It is okay to wonder why we feel alone. It is okay to wonder why He is allowing bad things to happen to us. It is okay to wonder why He isn't taking care of every part of our circumstance and removing our reason to fear.

We say with the psalmist David: "Save me, O God, for the waters have come up to my neck. I sink in the miry depths, where there is no foothold. I have come into the deep waters; the floods engulf me. I am worn out calling for help; my throat is parched. My eyes fail, looking for my God" (Psalm 69:1-3). In the midst of our fears, it is okay to wonder where God is. It is okay to ask God hard questions.

It is natural and normal to experience times of doubt when everything around us is falling apart. But during times like these, we must also reexamine our expectations of God and make sure they are not unrealistic. Often our expectation is that God will alleviate the circumstances that are causing our fear, but God never made that promise. He has promised to walk with us *through* our fear, but He has never promised to alleviate the cause for our fear. God has promised that we will never have to deal with anything alone, but He has not promised that we won't feel alone.

When Ralph went to his pastor, with his doubts, questions, and concerns, his pastor scolded him, "You must not think these things about God. You must not ask God these questions. You need to just realize that God is there."

"But my life is spinning out of control, and it feels like I am alone," countered Ralph.

"That is because you don't have enough faith," his pastor replied.

"Well, why is my wife leaving me? Why is my family falling apart?" Ralph continued.

"Maybe you weren't a good enough husband or father."

Needless to say, that wasn't the kind of thing that Ralph needed to hear and as he walked out of his pastor's office, he felt worse than he ever had in his life. Instead of feeling abandoned by his wife and thinking that God did not care, he now felt like the situation was all his own fault. He felt he needed to give himself the lion's share of the blame.

When you are in the midst of your fear, you do not need to hear platitudes of spirituality. You need to be allowed to cry out to God. We have talked about the stages of loss that we go through when our worst fears come true. Two of those stages are denial and anger. And when we are in the anger stage, we

171

are going to spend a lot of time talking to God, maybe even yelling at Him. We are going to ask God why He is letting this happen to us. But the good news is that we are not the only people who have done that. Some of the best examples of people who have cried out to God are found in the Bible, especially the Book of Psalms.

In my own life I find that when I am beset by fears and feel like God is not near, one of the best things I can do is open the Old Testament and listen to David and other poets. I hear them wondering where God is in the midst of their turmoil and trouble. I hear men who are desperately afraid of what is happening to them.

Overcoming our family fears will eventually lead us to God. Our first contact with God may be in our anger, disappointment, and sense of betrayal that He has allowed this to happen. It is okay to feel that way. If you have not had these feelings, you would not be human.

As a matter of fact, it may be a necessary step in coming to grips with family fears. Many of us have been brought up in homes and traditions of faith where we were taught not to express negative emotions to God. Yet one look at the Books of Job, Psalms, Ecclesiastes, and Lamentations shows us that it is okay to cry out to God. He is bigger than our fear. He is bigger than our doubt. He is bigger than our sense of disappointment. Perhaps it is only through this doubt and sense of disappointment that we really will move on and get a sense that God is there and can help us.

To do this, we need to see both God and our circumstances in proper perspective. As Erwin Lutzer puts it in his book, *Managing Your Emotions:*

> Often the experiences we fear the most are actually acts of God. He is attempting to put His arms around us. That's why I can say with full assurance that Jesus is in the midst of your fear. The misinterpretation, the misunderstanding that has come to you as a result of that fear can be dissipated when you realize that Jesus Christ is in

172

the midst of it, just as He was in the midst of the disciples' fear. There is something else you must understand if you are to get the proper perspective on your fear. Not only is Jesus Christ in the midst of your fear, but He also knows what your fear is all about and the feelings it gives you (Victor Books, 1983, p. 71).

Matthew 14 gives the account of Jesus' disciples being out on the lake when a storm came up. The disciples were afraid. They looked around, and they felt as though the boat would sink as the waves crashed about them. As the wind grew and the water washed over the decks, they were sure that they were about to drown, and the fear almost overwhelmed them. Then one of them looked and there in the middle of the tempest, in the middle of the storm, was Jesus. And His words to them in the midst of their fear are His words to us in the midst of ours: "Take courage! It is I. Don't be afraid" (Matthew 14:27). We need to see Jesus in the midst of our fear.

You may not be able to do it that way right now. The fears that you have for your family may be controlling you. They may be driving you. They may be the most powerful force in your life. And as you are surrounded by the storm of these fears, you don't see Jesus. All you see is the wind and the waves. But know this, He has promised to be there in the midst of your deepest, darkest night. He has promised to be a light in your nightmare. He has promised that in the middle of the storm He will be there, and His words to you ring out across 2,000 years of time just as they did to the disciples in that boat. "It is I. Don't be afraid." Our God is the God who stood with Shadrach, Meshach, and Abednego in the furnace of fire. It was in their moment of testing that they met God. It was in their moment of greatest distress and fear that He was with them and made himself known to them. As the song writer Rich Mullins puts it, "You will meet God in the furnace a long time before you meet Him in the air."

You will sense His presence and His love in the furnace of

your fear in a way that is not possible when life is going well. It is when we are at our lowest point, when the fire is licking at our toes and the fear is surrounding us that we will see Jesus walking toward us with His arms outstretched. "It is I. Do not be afraid."

We need to rely on four powerful things from God:

☐ God's providence
☐ God's promises
☐ God's presence
☐ God's power

God's Providence

God's providence means that the world and our lives are not ruled by the whims of fate, chance, or random luck. When our world spins out of control and fear has us in its grip, we must remember the world is not out of God's control; He is God. He is in control. He is working His will in creation, and He is revealing Himself in our lives. In the midst of our fears we need to know that even though we cannot control what is happening, the bad things in our lives are not random bad luck. It is all a part of God's working in this world. God's providence tells us that we are not subject to the petty whims of fate, but instead we are in providential relationship to God. Everything that happens to us in our families, everything that we fear and worry about, all of these things are under God's care.

That may not sound too comforting. If right now the things that you feared most in your life have come to pass, hearing someone tell you that God is in control sounds pretty empty. It is more than a platitude. It is a fact that we have to get a grip on to overcome our fears. These things are happening for a bigger purpose, one that we may not ever understand. We need to learn to rely on God's providence concerning our spouses and our children. As the Apostle Paul writes, "He is before all things, and in Him all things hold together" (Colossians 1:17).

God's Promises

We also must learn to rely on God's promises. Hebrews 13, verses 5 and 6 say, "Be content with what you have, because God has said, 'Never will I leave you; never will I forsake you.' So we say with confidence, 'The Lord is my helper; I will not be afraid. What can man do to me?' " God does not lie. If He lied, He would not be God. If He could not live up to His promises, He could not be God. And this God is the One who has made the universe, the God who set the planets in motion, put the stars in the sky, set the sun in the heavens. He has said to us, "Never will I leave you; never will I forsake you."

You may be worried and concerned about what is happening to your children, but you do not need to be afraid because nothing can change the fact that God will never leave you, even in the middle of your darkest night.

You may feel that your husband does not care for you anymore and be worried about your marriage, but do not let your fear consume you because God has promised that He will never leave you and that He will never forsake you. As the psalmist David said, "Even as I walk through the valley of the shadow of death . . . You are with me" (Psalm 23:4). As you walk through the valley of the shadow of your fear and as it rises up and claws at you, seeking to gain control of your life, God is with you. He has promised never to leave you alone. He has promised that when times are tough, He will come alongside and even carry you. He is there.

A few years ago, I was camping with my brother and best friend in northern Michigan near Sleeping Bear Dunes National Lakeshore. One of the dunes there overlooks Lake Michigan, with a steep path that drops nearly 500 feet to the lake. It is a beautiful sight with the waves crashing on the shore and the wind blowing in from the west. A sign posted at the beginning of this path reads: "Do not run down this dune. The climb up is extremely strenuous." But, of course, being young men with dubious judgment, we looked at each other and decided that we needed to run down the dune. We hopped the fence and began dashing headlong down this dune, rolling and falling because it was so steep. We had enormous fun, but I began to realize that we had made a bad choice when I got tired on the way down.

After we reached the bottom and walked around for a few minutes, we knew that we should not delay the climb back much longer, as the sun was already starting its way down and night was quickly approaching. So we began to climb back up the dune. First we tried walking straight up, and then we used our hands and finally we crawled. Being in the worst physical shape of the three, I had the most trouble. By the time I was a quarter of the way up the dune, I was exhausted and sick to my stomach. My legs felt like spaghetti, and my muscles had given out. After managing to haul my body about halfway up, I lay down, made a little hole for myself in the sand, and closed my eyes.

My friend Rob and my brother came alongside and wondered what was the matter with me. I said, "I am not going to make it, guys. I am so tired."

"We know you're tired. We're tired too. This dune is huge, and we should have never done this."

"No, you don't understand. I am really not going to make it. I cannot climb another step. Just leave me here." They looked at me for a moment, looked at each other, leaned forward, put their arms around me and staggered ten feet up the dune. We all fell over. They put their arms around me again, and we staggered ten more feet. We did this for 250 feet until we got to the top of the dune. We all lay there, gasping for breath, thankful to have made it to the top.

As we lay there, I looked at my brother and my friend and said, "Why did you carry me all the way up this dune?"

"Don't you know?" asked Rob.

"No! Why did you expend all of your energy helping me? Why did you sacrifice yourself for me?"

"You really don't know? You're my friend."

"I am your friend too, Rob, but I'm telling you, I would

have left you on the dune. I would not have had the strength to help you."

Rob replied, "Don't you understand, Jack? We carried you up the dune because we love you and we could never leave you."

When you feel like I did on that dune, Jesus will put His arms around you and pick you up. You can't make it to the top without Him. When you gain some perspective, you will see that you would have died there in your fear. Your fear would have controlled you, conquered you, owned you. But Jesus didn't leave you there. He carried you through your fear. Why? Because He loves you and has promised never to leave you or forsake you.

God's Presence

This brings us to the third thing we need to rely on: God's presence. His promise is that He will never leave us and inherent in this promise is His presence in our lives when we most need Him. God will not leave us to face our fear alone. According to Matthew 28:20, Jesus promised His disciples, "And surely, I am with you always, to the very end of the age." We question that. We wonder if God is with us when our daughter is pregnant, when our son is rebelling, when our dreams for our children are falling by the wayside. Jesus tells us that He is indeed with is, that He is with us to the ends of our fear, in our fear, and through our fear.

In Psalm 139 we learn the extent of God's presence in our lives:

> For You created my inmost being; You knit me together in my mother's womb. I praise You because I am fearfully and wonderfully made; Your works are wonderful, I know that full well. My frame was not hidden from You when I was made in the secret place. When I was woven together in the depths of the earth, Your eyes saw my unformed body. All the days ordained for me were writ-

ten in Your book before one of them came to be" (vv. 13-16).

Earlier in the same psalm David wrote,

O Lord, You have searched me and You know me. You know when I sit and when I rise; You perceive my thoughts from afar. You discern my going out and my lying down; You are familiar with all my ways. Before a word is on my tongue You know it completely, O Lord. You hem me in, behind and before; You have laid Your hand upon me (vv. 1-5).

God is there. His presence gives us comfort. We know that when the fear is too much for us to handle, we don't have to handle it alone.

God's Power

God's power is made strong in our weakness. Perhaps we are at our weakest when we are dominated by our fear. When fear is swirling about us, threatening our families, we are at our lowest. Then God comes in His power. The Apostle Paul wrote, "But He said to me, 'My grace is sufficient for you, for My power is made perfect in weakness.' Therefore I will boast all the more gladly about my weaknesses, so that Christ's power may rest on me. That is why, for Christ's sake, I delight in weaknesses, in insults, hardships, persecutions, in difficulties. For when I am weak, then I am strong" (2 Corinthians 12:9-10).

The God of the universe puts His power into us so we can say no when fear makes its play for control of our lives. God's power enables us to overcome the paralyzing effects of our family fears. God's power enables us to do the right thing when our fear is pushing us to do the wrong thing. God's power enables us to see Jesus in the midst of our fear even when we are surrounded by the wind and waves. It is God's power that enables us to keep going even when our worst fears come true.

It was God's power that enabled my family to make it when my brother came home with the shocking news that his girlfriend was pregnant. It is God's power that has enabled parents to keep going after the death of a child. It is God's power that will enable Ralph to keep going after his wife abandoned him and his family. God's power is strongest where we are weak.

Job was beset by fear. His difficulties far exceed any of ours. And Job wondered where God was in the middle of his fear. When he questioned God's power, God at last answered and let Job know just how powerful He was.

Then the Lord answered Job out of the storm. He said, "Who is this that darkens My counsel with words without knowledge? Brace yourself like a man; I will question you, and you shall answer Me. Where were you when I laid the earth's foundation? Tell Me, if you understand. Who marked off its dimensions? Surely you know! Who stretched a measuring line across it? On what were its footings set, or who laid its cornerstone—while the morning stars sang together and all the angels shouted for joy? Who shut up the sea behind doors when it burst forth from the womb, when I made the clouds its garment and wrapped it in thick darkness, when I fixed limits for it and set its doors and bars in place, when I said, "This far you may come and no farther; here is where your proud waves halt"? Have you ever given orders to the morning, or shown the dawn its place, that it might take the earth by the edges and shake the wicked out of it? The earth takes shape like clay under a seal, its features stand out like those of a garment (Job 38:1-14).

God can answer all of those questions with "I am the One." God has said His power will be in us when we most need it. God's providence, promises, presence, and power make a compelling case for us to learn to rely on Him. We know it is difficult, when surrounded by fear, to look for God. We know it is difficult when our families seem to be falling apart to realize God is there and that ultimately He is in control, but we will never overcome our fears on our own power and with our own ability.

It is only through learning to rely on God that we will be able to overcome our fears and live lives free of the guilt, shame, and controlling impulses that fear brings into our lives. It is only through standing on God's promises and His providence that we will be able to look at our lives in the proper perspective and know that when things are spinning out of control, God still reigns. It is only when we see God in our lives with His arm around us, helping us though our fear, that we are able to know we won't be broken when our children are making bad choices. We know God is helping us and carrying us through our fear.

CHAPTER TWELVE

Living with Our Fear, and Getting On with Our Lives

After reading through to the end of this book, you may be asking the question, "When are they going to tell me how to live without fear? When will I learn to completely beat my fears?" We don't believe it is possible to live without fear. Our goal for families is that they learn to manage their fears so that fears don't dominate their lives and cause them to act irrationally. It is our goal to help you understand the forces that are driving you in your parenting or in your marriage relationship. Hopefully the steps we have laid out in the last three chapters will help you bring your fear under control.

It is not possible to live completely free from worry and fear. It is in our nature as human beings to fear the unknown, to look ahead and see dark times and scary possibilities. That's okay. Being afraid isn't a sin, and it isn't going to wreck your family, unless you allow your fear to grow unchecked inside you. If you give fear free reign in your life, it will come to dominate your thoughts, your actions, your family, your whole life. The central premise of this book is that it doesn't have to be that way. By becoming aware of how our fears are causing us to act, how they are influencing our choices as parents and spouses, we can learn to handle our fear instead of it handling us.

Family Fears

■　　　■　　　■

Tim came to us a total wreck. He wasn't sleeping well, was irritable all the time, and found himself in constant arguments with his wife. Tim's relationship with his nineteen-year-old son was going downhill fast. Luke had dropped out of college and was spending most of his time at the beach with his friends. He didn't show any signs of ambition or desire to finish school and better his life.

Tim was a driven, type-A kind of guy who had seen success in every area of his life. Starting with a few borrowed dollars, he had parlayed that into a thriving, lucrative business. One of Tim's great regrets was that he had never attended college. It was a sore point with him, and he was more than a little insecure about his lack of education. His dream for his son was that Luke would go to school, get a degree in business, and return home to help his father run the family business, eventually taking it over when Tim retired.

It isn't working out that way, and Tim is beside himself. He can't believe that his son is just drifting along without purpose; Tim has never been without a clearly defined purpose in his life. So he tried to goad his son back into school; then he tried to force him back into school. He threatened, cajoled, begged, yelled, but his son just laughed at him. By the time we saw Tim, he was angry beyond belief. He was angry at Luke for failing him, angry at himself for failing as a parent, and angry at God for letting his dreams and prayers go unanswered. Yet in spite of all this evidence, Tim didn't know what was bothering him. After seeing him a few times, we asked him, "Do you think it's possible that you are afraid your son isn't going to turn out right? Is it possible that a lot of the anger you feel is coming from that fear?"

A light seemed to go on as he began to explore the possibility that fear was gaining control over him. We talked about how his efforts to control Luke and their failure had frustrated him and how that frustration was turning very quickly to anger. We talked for a long time, with Tim eventually admitting his fear and finally coming to understand it better. He named it, assessed the rationality of it, and weighed the risks to his son and his family if his fear was borne out.

Tim then walked through the steps we've outlined for you and began to see all the little ways his fear was actually driving his son away. He changed the way he dealt with Luke, trying to do only what he could do and letting Luke take responsibility for his life. He turned to God and found that God had not forsaken him or given up on his family. In fact, he began to feel God's love and protection in a new way.

Tim isn't the same person anymore. Luke isn't following his father's plan for his life, but that isn't driving Tim any more. He has let go of the idea that he can control his son and found that release to be the most freeing experience of his life. "I still wonder where Luke is going with his life. But it's kind of funny. Since I've relaxed, he's been talking about going back to school, and now he has a decent job. I'm still worried about him, but I know that I can't make his choices for him. I can't live his life for him. And I feel pretty good about that. It definitely feels better than letting my fear drive everyone away."

■　　　■　　　■

You and I can find the same peace that Tim has found. It's not easy, and it takes time to relinquish control and let our fears subside. It can happen if you choose to make it happen. Our fear isn't going to go away miraculously. Instead, we'll slowly gain ground on it when we decide that it isn't going to control us or our families anymore. When we begin to take responsibility for managing our fear and follow the simple, yet very difficult steps to bring that fear under control, we will experience freedom that we never dreamed possible. To regain control of our lives is perhaps the best feeling in the world, and to gain a mastery over our fear is the only way to do it.

Decide right now whether you are going to allow fear to run

your life for even one more day. Decide what you can do about it and make a plan. We know you can do it. We've had to handle fear in our own lives, and we have seen many families put fear behind them, moving into a new, vibrant, exciting relationship with each other and with God.

Family Fears
Video Curriculum Kit

Produced by Gospel Films, each kit contains everything you need for a Sunday School class, retreat, or family viewing series:

- [ ] 1 copy of *Family Fears*
- [ ] 4-part/4-session video
- [ ] 1 leader's guide

Priced at $79.95 (Catalog No. 3-1221)

Available at your local Christian bookstore